Henry Bleckly

Socrates and the Athenians

Henry Bleckly

Socrates and the Athenians

ISBN/EAN: 9783743316249

Manufactured in Europe, USA, Canada, Australia, Japa

Cover: Foto ©ninafisch / pixelio.de

Manufactured and distributed by brebook publishing software (www.brebook.com)

Henry Bleckly

Socrates and the Athenians

SOCRATES AND
THE ATHENIANS

An Apology

BY

HENRY BLECKLY

LONDON
KEGAN PAUL, TRENCH & CO., 1 PATERNOSTER SQUARE
1884

To the Right Honourable

LORD WINMARLEIGH,

FOR MANY YEARS THE MOST HONOURED RESIDENT
OF WARRINGTON, THE FOLLOWING PAGES,
CONTRIBUTED TO THE PROCEEDINGS OF
"THE WARRINGTON LITERARY AND
PHILOSOPHICAL SOCIETY," ARE,

BY PERMISSION, INSCRIBED.

SOCRATES AND THE ATHENIANS.

THE present inhabitants of Greece, whether they be the descendants of that imperial race which once occupied the country, or whether they be the posterity of those barbarous tribes which subsequently despoiled and depopulated it, are said to feel that they lie under some sort of obloquy and opprobrium on account of the judicial condemnation and death of Socrates, for which the Greece of more than 2000 years ago made itself responsible; and it has been suggested that in some Court or other a motion should be made for a new trial, and that the cause should be re-heard. The verdict of the civilized world has not confirmed and approved the verdict of Athens; at least, it has not done so with anything like unanimity. It is true there have been writers who have defended Athens; but it is most material, if we would pass a fair judgment upon the case, that we should regard it from the point of view of contemporaries. How did it come to pass that two such admittedly intelligent forces were brought into conflict? What was it that caused the collision? and how did it happen that it resulted so disastrously? It is easy to denounce the Athenians and to exonerate Socrates, and it is not difficult to extenuate Athens and to blame Socrates. Modern criticism has done both. Counsel has been heard on behalf of Socrates and on behalf of Athens; and another age, uninfluenced by the passions and prejudices which prevailed when the cause was first tried, have reconsidered the facts and the pleadings, and have decided it, some in one way and some in another. There is no new evidence to be adduced on the subject; no new facts or documents have been brought to light. What Plato and Xenophon said at the time is the most authentic information which remains; but each generation is apt to look at the evidence from its own point of view. What is really wanted is that we should put ourselves as far as possible in the position of the actors in this drama, making all due allowance for the feelings, the temper, and the prejudices of those who were concerned in the transaction; and we must remember that what is called prejudice by a later generation was very often by a contemporary one denominated by the word "principle," or by some other equally eulogistic name. That which in one man or one era is a real and strong prejudice, is only discovered to have been so when the man is dead and the era has passed away. A few years ago it was hardly possible for an Englishman who was not a Greek scholar to make himself acquainted with the true history of Socrates as it presented itself to the Athenian people. The works of Plato were practically inaccessible to English readers, and a real history of Greece, depicting the institutions, character, surroundings, and mental condition of its people, was not within the reach of an ordinary English reader. All this has now been reversed. The Master of Balliol College, Oxford (Professor Jowett), has published a translation of Plato's works, with copious introductions, which enable an English reader to appreciate the Socratic dialogue, even if many of its beauties are lost in the process of translation. This work is in our own Free Library; and though some of the dialogues may seem trifling and tedious, those relating to the trial and death of Socrates ought to be read by everyone. Then the "History of Greece," by George Grote, is a picture of the Greek people such as no Englishman ever produced before. It is the work of a man who brought before his own mind and presented to his readers the many phases of Greek life and the various phenomena which marked and distinguished that remarkable people and made them what they were. Grote was an English politician, a member of Parliament, a man of profound culture and attainments, and a practical London banker, possessing warm and wide sympathies. To him the Greeks were living men, not dim and remote shadows; and the events of their history and the springs of action operating upon them were as familiar to him as the things of his daily life. He felt and appreciated their struggles and aspirations; and so his history has about it a vivacity and reality which stamp it in vivid colours upon the reader's mind. No picture of Socrates can be more distinct and clear than that which is drawn by Grote. It bears the impress of impartiality and truth, doing justice, as one must think, to the Athenian people, and not less so to Socrates. I can only gather from these and other sources the facts which relate to the history of Socrates, and place them before you in such a way as seems to me to give a fair, though it must necessarily be a very meagre, outline of them. Political and judicial institutions in all ages have been imperfect and fallible. Men in all ages, however excellent and well intentioned, have been the creatures of their own era; and if here and there one man has happened to rise above his own age, his fellow-men have usually regarded him with suspicion and antagonism. The man and the institutions have come into conflict, and the weaker—the individual—has usually gone to the wall. We may pass over so much of the personal history of Socrates as does not concern his philosophical character. There is no dispute about the events of his life, and there is not much to distinguish them from that of an ordinary Athenian. He served his country as a soldier, and performed those ordinary public duties which were expected of a man in his position, though he did not seek public employment. It is his philosophy and the peculiar methods by which he illustrated and enforced it that have distinguished him from the rest of his countrymen; it was the mental and moral habits of the man which marked him out from the crowd; it was his originality and force of character which made him so illustrious; and what we have to consider is, how these especial characteristics of his manifested themselves, how they influenced and affected the Athenian people, and how the conflict between them originated, and at last culminated in so fatal a manner. In order to understand this, we must try to make out what sort of man Socrates was, what sort of people and institutions it was amongst which he lived, and how it was they came to be placed in such antagonism to each other.

The greatness of Athens may be dated from about 500 years before our era. The battle of Marathon was fought 490 years B.C.; and the battle of Marathon may be reckoned as the opening act of that great drama which unfolded the power and glory of Athens. The victory thus achieved over the vast forces of Persia was one of those events which form the landmarks of history, and it roused a patriotic pride in the minds of the

Greek people which sustained them through long and desperate conflicts, and which, in fact, never wholly died out. Contemporaneously with this military greatness there was developed an intellectual and political greatness such as the world has never seen before or since. Athens rolled back the tide of Persian invasion, and her military success was followed by intellectual triumphs not less marvellous. There may have been in the history of the world poets, orators, philosophers, statesmen, and artists individually equal to the most eminent of the Greeks; but there has nowhere been a group of men, belonging to the same time and place, who could compare with them. The population of Athens was that of only a moderate provincial town in England, but it produced during the era of which we are speaking, not here and there a star of the first magnitude, but a whole constellation—artistic, philosophical, poetical—which continues to this day the most brilliant and distinguished in the intellectual firmament.

> While kings in dusty darkness hid,
> Have left a nameless pyramid,
> Thy heroes, though the general doom
> Hath swept the column from their tomb,
> A mightier monument command—
> The mountains of their native land!
> There points thy Muse to strangers' eye
> The graves of those who cannot die!

Much of the work done at this period in Greece has been lost. Statues and temples and columns have disappeared, but enough remain to prove the pre-eminent power that existed; poetry has passed into oblivion. Dramas innumerable have left only a name, but some few, tragic and comic, have escaped the ravages of time, and are universally held to be of unmatched beauty and excellence. Æschylus, Sophocles, Euripides, Aristophanes, would each have made any literature famous; and they all appeared, with competitors, who surpassed them, on the stage of Athens at the same period. The historians of later times acknowledge that Greek models are unapproachable, and the world's orators unanimously give precedence to those of Greece.

We may form some notion of a people whom we have not seen when we come to know their habits, pursuits, and amusements. If a people find pleasure in killing and tormenting animals, in bull-baiting, or cock-fighting, or sports of this kind, we may safely conclude that they are gross and barbarous. On the other hand, a people may prove by their amusements that they are frivolous and foolish. The Athenians do not come under any category of this kind.

The Greeks may be said to have created the theatre, and to have forthwith put upon the stage the most consummate series of dramas which have ever illustrated the dramatic art. The theatre at Athens was a national institution. It was provided for the whole male population. Thirty thousand persons, it is said, could be accommodated in it, and tickets were freely issued to those who were not able to buy them. Such a theatre was, of course, very little like ours. The performance took place in the daytime, under the open sky; there could be no roof to so vast a building; it was circular in form, the seats raised one above another so that all could hear and see. Very different and immensely inferior are the dramas which attract modern audiences. The Romans built places of amusement on the same model in form and style, and they devoted them to conflicts between wild beasts and to gladiatorial shows. The contrast between the Greeks and the Romans in this respect is as that between light and darkness, between barbarism and civilization. The amusement of the Greeks was of an intellectual order; that of the Romans was brutal and savage. Theatrical performance with the Greeks was associated with their religious feasts, and was originally devoted to the service of one of their gods.

When we are estimating the Athenian people it is essential that we should remember the points in which they differed from their neighbours, the nations which surrounded them, and the nations which followed in their wake—Egyptians, Babylonians, Carthaginians,

Romans. The poetry and philosophy of Athens could only have flourished among a highly-cultivated and intellectual people, and what they knew and what they did was of their own growth. They had no predecessors, and they have had no successors. The men who lived hundreds of years after them might criticize and condemn them, but in many things they have never yet reached their level, as we may further see by-and-bye. We judge of a man by his actions and conduct, by the books he reads, by his style of thought, and by the coarseness or refinement of his language. We judge of a nation by its literature, its laws, its intelligence, and its humanity. The Greek language is allowed by all to be an instrument of incomparable power and precision. Greek thought has been the most influential, far-reaching, and vivifying which the world has known; and we may safely infer that the people who created and used such an apparatus, and for such high purposes, stood in the very first rank. What they were politically is a question which may be postponed; but here again they worked out problems of government more worthily than their contemporaries or predecessors. If their methods were imperfect and their success incomplete, they at least were pioneers of self-government, if they did not themselves permanently attain it. There was a very strenuous political life at Athens; and politics, even in this 19th century of grace, and in this intelligent and Christian England of ours, is not always a school of moderation and good manners, of good temper and generous feeling and polite language. It is not the fashion even now among political partisans to put the best construction upon their opponent's acts, or to regard his faults with forbearance and kindliness; and therefore if it is alleged against the Athenians that the oligarchical Socrates when brought to trial was obnoxious to a turbulent democracy, we must not deny to the Athenians as jurymen the instinct of fair play, unless we are prepared at the same time to acknowledge that our own politics have eaten out entirely the very heart and vitals of our judicial faculty and feeling. Let it be admitted that the Athenians, though they were hard hitters, could and did when they entered the jury box leave behind them political malevolence.

There is another most important factor in the history of the Athenians which we must consider, if we would do justice between Socrates and his judges. The accusation against Socrates was that he was not loyal to the religion of his country: the specific charge will come out by-and-bye. We must not suppose that because the religion of the Athenians seems to us extravagant and absurd that it therefore had no hold upon the feelings and thoughts of the Athenians themselves. It is very easy for people who look at a religion which has passed away, and which possessed innumerable gods, to speak of it slightly and contemptuously; but this is not doing justice to it. What we have to ask is, how did those people regard their religion? Did it affect their minds? Did it move their feelings? Did it create fear and hope, and joy and terror? If it did, then it was a potent agent and a powerful influence which overshadowed their life. It might be full of folly and falsehood, but it might be not the less real in its operation. When we are thinking of a religion which existed thousands of years ago we are not to judge of it by what it *seems* now, but by what it *was* then—by its effects. Did it sometimes create alarm and sometimes kindle hope? for if it did, however unreasonable it may now seem, it was once a living agency that influenced men. That this was the character of the Greek religion is clear. It had religious services of all sorts, and it was woven up with all the events of Greek life. The age of which we are speaking was not an age of books, but of teaching by the living voice, by poetry and mythical romances which were recited by impassioned speakers, whose narratives were received with unquestioning faith, and became the staple of the national religion. The stories of Homer were the quarry from which the religion of Greece was shaped and fashioned. Homer, it has been said, was the Bible of the Greeks. Professor Mahaffy, in his "Social Life in Greece," says:

"To the old-fashioned Athenian, his mythology was the source of his morals and of his highest culture. He had framed for himself ideals of bravery, of honour, and of greatness from his Homer; he had seen the tragic poets draw their most splendid inspiration from these legends; he had seen the Epos inspire the painter, the sculptor, and the architect—in fact, the whole glory of Athens, literary, social, and artistic, was bound up with the Homeric theology. Supposing him, therefore, to be persuaded by the philosophers, and to abandon in secret the faith of his forefathers, we can well imagine him arguing, with even more apparent force than the modern sceptic, that, however false or fictitious were these ancient legends, however unproved or doubtful this ancient creed, yet at all events under it, and through it, Athens had grown in splendour, and become perfect in culture—that, therefore, no citizen versed in the annals of Athens, and appreciating her true greatness, could venture to speak disrespectfully of her creed, even were it proved to be obsolete."

The gentlemen assembled at Xenophon's Symposium express themselves satisfied with their faith, and Xenophon tells them that the gods inform him, by signs, voices, dreams, and omens, what he should do and forbear, and that when he obeys them he never has reason to repent. Socrates replies, "None of these things are the least incredible; but this I should like to hear, how you serve them so as to make them such friends of yours." "So you shall," is the reply, "and I do it at a very moderate expense, for I praise them without any cost to myself, and of what they grant me I always return them a share. I speak of them respectfully as far as I can, and when I call them to witness, I never intentionally tell a lie." "Well, by Jove!" says Socrates, "if by so doing you have the gods your friends, the gods too, it seems, are pleased with gentlemanly conduct."

We may think ourselves much better than Xenophon; but what we have to consider is that, with all its apparent absurdity in the eyes of this 19th century, it was 2000 or 3000 years ago an institution which challenged the homage and directed the movements and feelings of intelligent men. We must never forget that what is folly and nonsense to one age may be a most potent and governing influence in another. If the mythology of Greece were not an agency of this kind, then the case against Socrates was stronger than at first it may appear. He was accused of a sort of impiety, of disregarding and disbelieving in his country's gods. He, in fact, denied this allegation, and contended that in truth he was a sincere worshipper. He claimed to associate himself with his countrymen in his regard and reverence for their common divinities. Was this true or not? Socrates, by his defence, admitted that the people of Athens had certain recognised gods whom they worshipped, and he asserted that he was a fellow-worshipper with them. We must not, therefore, assume, because they were polytheists, that they had no real religion, or that the religion they professed had no hold upon their feelings. What we have to remember is, that religion with the Athenians was, perhaps, not associated with a lofty and pure morality out of which it grew and which sustained it, but that mainly it manifested itself in ceremonies, feasts, sacrifices, invocations, and a variety of acts intended to propitiate, to appease, or to please their divinities. These acts were visible, palpable things; and so long as a man performed them according to custom he was safe. I lay some stress on this, for reasons which will hereafter appear; and there is one other piece of evidence which I wish to produce before quitting this part of the subject. St Paul visited Athens 300 or 400 years after the death of Socrates. Religion in the meantime had not taken deeper root in Athens; indeed, it had lost much of its hold upon the more educated people; but St Paul said, addressing a body of Athenians, "I perceive that in all things ye are too superstitious, for as I passed by and beheld your devotions, I saw an altar," &c. Now this word "superstition" means generally, an expectation of supernatural results, by means incompetent or absurd. Shakespeare uses the word in this sense. Addressing Pericles, one of the sailors says : " Sir, your queen must overboard ; the sea works high, the wind is loud, and will not lie till the ship be cleared of the dead." To which Pericles replies : " That's your superstition ; " and the sailor responds : " Pardon us, sir ; with us on sea it hath been still observed ; and we are strong in custom." There was no real connection between throwing the dead body overboard and the ceasing of the storm, but the sailors had been brought up to think there was ; and as this was a mere delusion it is properly called superstition. St Paul tells the Athenians in his time that they were in all things too superstitious—that is, they expected to gain certain ends or attain special objects through some religious instrumentality, which was altogether irrational ; and on this account he called them superstitious ; and he connects it with their devotions, so that it is clear he recognised the acts which they performed in connection with their altars as religious acts, for he calls them devotions. He implies, nevertheless, that the acts, however well meant on their part, were futile, and could not accomplish the effects which were intended, but, on the contrary, were mere superstitions. My construction of this statement is, that the Athenians in the time of St Paul continued to be a religious people after their fashion and in the sense of performing religious acts, in honour of

B

or propitiatory of certain superior beings whom they called gods, and that this superstitious state of mind had a strong and lively hold upon their feelings.

We have, then, at Athens in the time of Socrates a highly intellectual people, self-governed, and impressed with religious or superstitious feelings; and there is another point which must also be mentioned. St Paul at the same time said of the Athenians that they were always seeking after new things. Anterior to the battle of Marathon the national life was comparatively undeveloped; they were governed by old traditions, and the history of their gods and their own religious ideas were not subjects of inquiry. What was contained in the teaching of their poets they clung to without investigation; but there came a new race of poets, and there sprung up philosophers who wanted to know the origin and cause of everything, and the sentiments of the poets and the discussions of the philosophers created doubts which disturbed many quiet people. These people—and clever people they were—did not like the new style of talking and the new ideas. They preferred the old-fashioned ways and days, when no one questioned their customs or the stories connected with their gods. There was, therefore, a considerable gulf between one set of Athenians and another on the subject of religion. But the characteristic of the Athenians, that they sought after new things, prevented these matters going to sleep, and in various ways—upon the stage and in the schools of the philosophers—the religion of the country was disparaged, and was losing its hold upon the better educated classes. Amongst this keen-witted, superstitious, inquisitive, and fermenting people Socrates lived. He seems to have followed no occupation, but to have devoted himself to the teaching and instruction of the people in his own peculiar and original manner. The Athenians lived out of doors, and Socrates in all public places devoted himself to the one occupation of interrogating and conversing with whoever was willing to talk with him. We must read Plato's Dialogues if we would understand the Socratic method. Early in the morning Socrates frequented the public walks, the gymnasia for bodily training, and the schools where the youth were receiving instruction. He was to be seen in the market-place at the hour when it was most crowded; among the booths and tables where goods were exposed for sale; his whole day was usually spent in this public manner. He talked with anyone, young or old, rich or poor, who sought to address him, and in the hearing of all who chose to stand by. Not only he never either asked or received any reward, but he made no distinction of persons, never withheld his conversation from anyone, and talked upon general topics to all. He conversed with politicians, sophists, soldiers, artisans, and studious or ambitious youths. He visited all persons of interest in the city, male and female. Nothing could be more public, perpetual, and indiscriminate as to persons than his conversation. And as it was engaging, curious, and instructive to hear, certain persons were accustomed to attend him in public as companions and listeners. These men, a fluctuating body, were commonly known as his disciples or scholars; though neither he nor his personal friends ever employed the terms "teacher" and "disciple" to describe the relation between them. Many of them came, attracted by his reputation during the later years of his life, from other Grecian cities. No other person, so far as is known, in Athens or in any other Grecian city, appears to have manifested himself in this perpetual and indiscriminate manner as a public talker for instruction. All teachers either took money for their lessons or at least gave them apart from the multitude in a private house or garden to special pupils, with admissions and rejections at their own pleasure. By the peculiar mode of life which Socrates pursued, not only his conversation reached the minds of a much wider circle, but he became more widely known as a person. While acquiring a few attached friends and admirers, and raising a certain intellectual interest in others, he at the same time provoked a large number of personal enemies. This extreme publicity of life and conversation was one among the characteristics of Socrates, distinguishing him from all other teachers before or after. Next was his persuasion of a special religious mission, impulses and communications sent to him by the gods. Taking the belief of such intervention generally, it was indeed in no way peculiar to Socrates; it was the ordinary faith of the ancient world; and explanations of the phenomena of the world, resolving them into general laws, were regarded with disapprobation. Xenophon defends Socrates from the charge of religious innovation by asserting that he pretended to nothing which was not included in the creed of every pious man. But this is not precisely what Socrates said in his defence before the judges. He had been accustomed, he said, constantly to hear, even from his childhood, a divine voice, interfering at moments when he was about to act, in the way of restraint, but never in the way of instigation. Later writers speak of this as the dæmon or genius of Socrates, but he himself does not personify it, but treats it merely as a divine sign, a prophetic or supernatural voice. He was accustomed not only to obey it implicitly, but to speak of it publicly and familiarly to others, so that the fact was well known to his friends and to his enemies. Though his persuasion on the subject was unquestionably sincere and his obedience constant, yet he never dwelt upon it himself as anything grand or awful, or entitling him to peculiar deference, but spoke of it often in his usual strain of familiar playfulness. But to his enemies and to the Athenian public it appeared in the light of an offensive heresy, an impious innovation on the orthodox creed, and a desertion of the recognized gods of Athens. Such was the dæmon or genius of Socrates as described by himself, and as conceived in the genuine Platonic Dialogues—a voice always prohibiting and bearing exclusively upon his own personal conduct. That which Plutarch and other admirers of Socrates conceived as a dæmon or intermediate being between God and man was looked upon by the Fathers of the Christian Church as a devil, and by some moderns as mere ironical phraseology on the part of Socrates himself. But though this peculiar form of inspiration belonged exclusively to him, there were also other ways in which he believed himself to have received the special mandates of the gods. Such distinct mission had been imposed upon him by dreams, by oracular intimations, and by every other means which the gods employed for signifying their special will. In his defence he said: "My service to the god has not only constrained me to live in constant poverty and neglect of political estimation, but has brought upon me a host of bitter enemies in those whom I have examined and exposed, while the bystanders talk of me as a wise man, because they give me credit for wisdom respecting all the points on which my exposure of others turns. The difference between me and others is that I was fully conscious of my ignorance, whilst they were not; I was exempt from that capital error." Then he adds: " Whatever may be the danger and obloquy which I may incur, it would be monstrous, indeed, if, having maintained my place in the ranks as a soldier under your generals at Delium and Potideæ, I were now, from fear of death or anything else, to disobey the oracle and desert the post which the god has assigned to me, the duty of living for philosophy and cross-questioning both myself and others; and should you even now offer to acquit me, on condition of my renouncing this duty, I should tell you, with all respect and affection, that I will obey the god rather than you, and that I will persist until my dying day in cross-questioning you, exposing your want of wisdom and virtue, and reproaching you until the defect is remedied. My mission as your monitor is a mark of the special favour of the god to you, and if you condemn me it will be your loss, for you will find none other such. Perhaps you will ask me, 'Why, cannot you go away, Socrates, or live among us in peace and silence?' This is the hardest of all questions for me to answer to your satisfaction. If I tell you that silence on my part would be disobedience to the god, you will think me in jest, and not believe me. You will believe me still less if I tell you that the greatest blessing which can happen to a man is to carry on discussions every day about virtue and those other matters which you hear me canvassing when I cross-examine myself as well as others; and that life without such examination is no life at all. Nevertheless, so stands the fact, incredible as it may seem to you." This is the way in which Socrates defended himself before the judges as reported by Plato. It is plain evidence that he believed himself to be executing a supernatural mission which he felt himself compelled to follow. Nothing could well be more unpopular and obnoxious than the task which he undertook of cross-examining and convicting of ignorance every distinguished man whom he could approach. So violent, indeed, was the enmity which he occasionally provoked, that he was sometimes struck and maltreated, and frequently laughed to scorn. One cannot fail to be reminded, in reading the style of defence adopted by Socrates, of some words in the Acts of the Apostles, spoken before a Jewish tribunal, "Whether it be right in the sight of God to hearken to you more than to God, judge ye," and, "we cannot but speak." St Paul asks, "Am I become your enemy because I tell you the truth?" and then he says, "Necessity is laid upon me, and woe is me if I preach not." Stripped of any special signification, these expressions would convey the same meaning to the hearers, viz., that each of the speakers had, in his own opinion, some divine mission, and was, as it were, constrained to speak. The Athenians called St Paul a babbler, but they said also, "We would know what these things mean," and in this spirit they listened to Socrates; and the Apostle who stood upon Mars Hill and the philosopher with mean garments and ill-favoured features who addressed them daily in the streets were, no doubt, regarded at Athens as men of the same stamp, and we cannot but be struck through all the differences with a certain similarity which marks the one set of circumstances and the other, and we may say also with the same result, for each was subjected to violence. (Dislike of contradiction, unwillingness to consider and to treat with respect another man's point of view, determination to resist any modification of thought or feeling, and an obstinate adherence to unintelligent custom, have been characteristics not of men here and there, but of all sorts and conditions of men in nearly all climes and times.) When the men of Ephesus were foiled in argument, they overpowered their antagonists by force of lungs, shouting for the space of two hours, "Great is Diana of the Ephesians," and this sort of insensate shouting has often enough in the history of the world drowned the still small voice of reason and conscience in its appeals to men's better judgment and feelings.

But in order to be fair and just we must remember that Socrates and men of his stamp touch their contemporaries in a very tender part. Socrates admits that his mode of addressing his contemporaries was unpleasant to them, but then he alleges that it was a sort of medicine which was good for them. This they did not perceive; its present flavour and quality were disagreeable, and roused a feeling of hostility, and there did not exist at Athens, and there has not existed elsewhere amongst the common people generally, an openness of mind, a calmness of temper, and a judicial faculty which would enable them to weigh and measure the statements put before them. There has been no disposition to do this. "Am I become your enemy because I tell you the truth?" asks St Paul, but this in the main is what people did, and do think, whenever that which the speaker calls truth happens to conflict with what the hearer has been accustomed to consider the truth. If we would do justice to the Athenians we must take account of this general infirmity of mankind, and then we shall have to ask ourselves also whether the Athenians were more or less tenacious and intemperate in their opposition and resistance to new teachers than their neighbours. There was, then, this antagonism between Socrates and a large part of the Athenians, mixed up also, as it may be assumed, with some political feeling, of which there was not a little in Athens. Socrates, be it remembered, was one of that party who thought that the functions of government belonged legitimately to those who knew best how to exercise them for the good of the governed. The legitimate king or governor was not the man who held the sceptre, nor the man elected by some vulgar persons, nor he who had got the post by lot, nor he who had thrust himself in by force or fraud; but he alone who knew how to govern well ; just as the pilot governed on shipboard, and the surgeon in a sick man's house, and the trainer in the palæstra, simply because their greater knowledge was an admitted fact. It was absurd, Socrates contended, to choose political officers by lot, when no one would trust himself on shipboard under care of a pilot picked up by chance. Under these circumstances, a time came when his opponents determined to bring him before the tribunal, and the mode of doing it was this : Athens at that time was governed by ten Archons. One of these was called the King Archon, and his functions were almost all connected with religion. He was, as his title shows, the representative of the old kings in their capacity of high priest, and had to offer up sacrifices and prayer ;

moreover, indictments for impiety and similar offences were laid before him.

In the year 399 B.C., Melêtus, Anytus, and Lykon presented against Socrates, and hung up in the appointed place, the portico of the office of the King Archon, an indictment in the following terms: "Socrates is guilty of crime, first, for not worshipping the gods whom the city worships, but introducing new divinities of his own; next, for corrupting the youth. The penalty due is death." The matter and manner of this proceeding are brought before us vividly in the dialogue of Plato named "Euthyphro," the scene of which is the porch of the King Archon where Socrates meets Euthyphro, who commences the conversation thus (I take it from Jowett's translation) :—

Why have you left the Lyceum, Socrates; and what are you doing in the porch of the King Archon? Surely you are not engaged in an action before the King as I am.

Socrates. Not in an action, Euthyphro; indictment is the word the Athenians use.

Euth. What! I suppose some one has been prosecuting you, for I cannot believe that you are the prosecutor of another.

Soc. Certainly not.

Euth. Then some one else has been prosecuting you?

Soc. Yes.

Euth. And who is he?

Soc. A young man who is little known, Euthyphro; and I hardly know him. His name is Melêtus. Perhaps you may remember his appearance. He has a beak, and long straight hair, and a beard which is ill grown.

Euth. No, I do not remember him, Socrates. And what is the charge he brings against you?

Soc. What is the charge? Well, a very serious charge, which shows a great deal of character in the young man, and for which he is certainly not to be despised. He says he knows how the youth are corrupted and who are their corrupters. I fancy that he must be a wise man; and seeing that I am anything but a wise man, he has found me out, and is going to accuse me of corrupting his young friends. And of this our mother the State is to be the judge. Of all our political men he is the only one who seems to me to begin in the right way, with the cultivation of virtue in youth, and if he goes on as he has begun he will be a very great public benefactor.

Euth. I hope that he may, but I rather fear, Socrates, that the reverse will turn out to be the truth. My opinion is that in attacking you he is simply aiming a blow at the State in a sacred place. But in what way does he say that you corrupt the young?

Soc. He brings a wonderful accusation against me, which at first hearing excites surprise. He says that I am a poet or maker of gods, and that I make new gods and deny the existence of old ones. This is the ground of his indictment.

Euth. I understand, Socrates; he means to attack you about the familiar sign which occasionally, as you say, comes to you. He thinks that you are a neologian, and he is going to have you up before the Court for this. He knows that such a charge is readily received, for the world is always jealous of novelties in religion. And I know that when I myself speak in the Assembly about divine things, and foretell the future to them, they laugh at me as a madman; and yet every word that I say is true. But they are jealous of all of us. I suppose we must be brave and not mind them.

Soc. Their laughter, friend Euthyphro, is not a matter of much consequence. For a man may be thought wise; but the Athenians, I suspect, do not care much about this, until he begins to make other men wise; and then, for some reason or other—perhaps, as you say, from jealousy—they are angry.

Euth. I have no desire to try conclusions with them about this.

Soc. I dare say you don't make yourself common, and are not apt to impart your wisdom. But I have a benevolent habit of pouring out myself to everybody, and would even pay for a listener, and I am afraid the Athenians know this; and therefore, as I was saying, if the Athenians would only laugh at me as you say they laugh at you, the time might pass gaily enough in the court; but perhaps they may be in earnest, and then what the end may be you soothsayers only can predict.

Euth. I dare say the affair will end in nothing, Socrates, and that you will win your cause; and I think I shall win mine.

Soc. By the powers, Euthyphro! how little does the common herd know of the nature of right and truth!

Euth. And how little do they know, Socrates, of the opinions of the gods about piety and impiety.

Soc. Good Heavens, Euthyphro! have you any precise knowledge of piety and impiety, and of divine things in general?

Euth. The best of Euthyphro, and that which distinguishes him, Socrates, from other men, is his exact knowledge of all these matters.

Soc. Rare friend! I think I cannot do better than be your disciple before the trial with Melêtus comes on. Then I shall challenge him, and say that I have always had a great interest in all religious questions, and now, as he charges me with rash imaginations and innovations in religion, I have become your disciple. I suppose that people think me wrong because I cannot believe all the current stories about the gods. But as you are so well informed about them and approve them, I cannot do better than assent to your superior wisdom. What else can I do, confessing as I must that I know nothing of them? I wish you would tell me whether you really believe that they are true.

Euth. Yes, Socrates; and things more wonderful still of which the world is in ignorance.

Soc. And do you really believe that the gods fought with one another, and had dire quarrels, battles, and the like, as the poets say, and as you may find represented in the works of great artists? The temples are full of them; and notably the robe of Athene, which is carried up to the Acropolis at the great Panathenæa, is embroidered with them. Are all these tales of the gods true, Euthyphro?

Euth. Yes, Socrates.

The conversation is carried on much further, until Euthyphro says at last:—

I really do not know, Socrates, how to say what I mean, for somehow or other our arguments, on whatever ground we rest them, seem to turn round and walk away.

Euthyphro was one of those superficial and self-satisfied people who are as numerous in the world now as they were then. Socrates flatters his vanity in order that he may convince him of his ignorance; but he does not succeed, and the conversation ends as it began, leaving Euthyphro with the same good opinion of himself. The dialogue shows us that there was, in the conversation of Socrates, what was likely to create distrust and dissatisfaction among those who believed without inquiry all the stories they had learned about the gods, and this feeling was at the bottom of the opposition to Socrates.

The change which was making itself felt in Athens during what may be called the Socratic period is visible in the writings of her poets and philosophers. Æschylus looks at human affairs from the standpoint of those mysterious powers which filled the early world with fear and terror; Sophocles tones down this austerity; Euripides introduces yet more largely the human element, and disparages much which was reckoned divine. Mrs Browning has described their characteristics in a very general way.

> Oh, our Æschylus the thunderous,
> How he drove the bolted breath
>   Through the cloud, to wedge it ponderous
> In the gnarled oak beneath!
>   Oh, our Sophocles the loyal,
> Who was born to monarch's place,
>   And who made the whole world royal
> Less by kingly power than grace!
>   Our Euripides, the human,
> With his droppings of warm tears,
>   And his touches of things common,
> Till they rose to touch the spheres!

The older-fashioned Athenians regarded Euripides

with suspicion. The new aspects which he introduced, the freer handling which he adopted, unsettled the traditions and beliefs which formerly ruled at Athens; and there was thus a large party with whom Euripides was unpopular. The feeling of this party was embodied in the fierce ridicule of Aristophanes. We may judge of the growth of new notions by comparing Æschylus with Euripides, but the invective of Aristophanes brings into much stronger contrast the difference that actually existed. No doubt Aristophanes was a violent caricaturist, but he was the mouthpiece of a party which clung to that past which Euripides and his party were prone to discredit. We are thinking of Socrates, we are thinking of his accusers, we are thinking of the charge of impiety brought against him, and we must take account of the contest which was being waged at the time between the old thought and the new, and neither was wholly good or wholly bad. Aristophanes exaggerated, but we may be sure there was a basis of reality in his caricatures. Many people believed that the men with whom Socrates associated were such as Aristophanes depicted, and it is men' beliefs which lead to actions. Aristophanes wrote a comedy called the "Clouds," which was acted in Athens some twenty years before the trial of Socrates, and he wrote it for the express purpose of holding up Socrates to public ridicule. I will read you part of a scene from this play, from which you will see in what light Socrates was exhibited to his fellow-citizens, and what sort of an opinion so keen an intellect as that of Aristophanes formed of him and his teaching. It must be remembered that Socrates and Aristophanes were on friendly terms, though it seems rather surprising that they should be.

The theatre of Athens, as we are told, held an audience of 30,000 persons, and the science and skill of Greek artists furnished all manner of contrivances which gave effect to the performance. In the scene from which I make my extract there are only two persons on the stage, Socrates and Strepsiades, and by some means clouds are represented which fulfil the part of the chorus—a very important part of a Greek play. The scene introduces us to Socrates. Strepsiades is a stupid sort of Athenian, in debt and difficulty, who has determined to visit what he called "the thought shop," to learn the new logic which he hopes will enable him to cheat his creditors. He knocks loudly at the door, which is opened to him, and being admitted, a conversation intended to ridicule the new notions takes place, the clouds, as the chorus, joining in it. The chorus has just spoken, and Strepsiades exclaims:—

Streps. Oh Earth! what a sound, how august and profound! it fills me with wonder and awe.

Soc. These, these then alone, for true Deities own, the rest are all God-ships of straw.

Streps. Let Zeus be left out : He's a God beyond doubt :
come, that you can scarcely deny.
Soc. Zeus, indeed! there's no Zeus: don't you be so obtuse.
Streps. No Zeus up aloft in the sky :
Then you first must explain, who it is sends the rain ;
or I really must think you are wrong.
Soc. Well, then, be it known, these send it alone : I can
prove it by arguments strong.
Was there ever a shower seen to fall in an hour
when the sky was all cloudless and blue ?
Yet on a fine day, when the Clouds are away, he
might send one, according to you.
Streps. Well, it must be confessed that chimes in with the
rest : your words I am forced to believe.
Yet before I had dreamed that the rain-water
streamed from Zeus and his wonderful sieve.
But whence then, my friend, does the thunder descend ?
that does make me quake with affright !
Soc. Why ! 'tis they, I declare, as they roll through the air.
Streps. What the Clouds ? did I hear you aright ?
Soc. Ay : for when to the brim filled with water they
swim, by Necessity carried along,
They are hung up on high in the vault of the sky,
and so by Necessity strong
In the midst of their course, they clash with great
force, and thunder away without end.
Streps. But it is not He who compels this to be ? does not
Zeus this Necessity send ?
Soc. No Zeus have we there, but a Vortex of air.
Streps. What ! Vortex ? that's something, I own.
I knew not before, that Zeus was no more, but
Vortex was placed on his throne ?
But I have not yet heard to what cause you referred
the thunder's majestical roar.
Soc. Yes, 'tis they, when on high full of water they fly,
and then, as I told you before,

          By Compression impelled, as they clash, are compelled a terrible clatter to make.

Streps. Well, but tell me from Whom comes the bolt through the gloom, with its awful and terrible flashes;
          And wherever it turns, some it singes and burns, and some it reduces to ashes!
          For this 'tis quite plain, let who will send the rain, that Zeus against perjurers dashes.

Soc. And how, you old fool of a dark-ages school, and an antediluvian wit,
          If the perjured they strike, and not all men alike, have they never Cleonymus hit?
          Then of Simon again, and Theorus explain: known perjurers yet they escape,
          But he smites his own shrine with these arrows divine, and 'Sunium, Attica's cape,'
          And the ancient gnarled oaks: now what prompted those strokes?
          They never forswore I should say.

Streps. Can't say that they do: your words appear true. Whence comes then the thunderbolt, pray?

Soc. When a wind that is dry, being lifted on high, is suddenly pent into these,
          It swells up their skin, like a bladder, within, by Necessity's changeless decrees;
          Till compressed very tight, it bursts them outright, and away with an impulse so strong,
          That at last by the force and the swing of its course, it takes fire as it whizzes along.

We have seen Socrates at the porch of the King Archon, and we have heard what he had to say about the prosecution. We must now inquire what sort of a tribunal it was before which he was arraigned.

SOCRATES AND THE ATHENIANS. 37

At Athens, in the time of Socrates, 6000 citizens were elected annually under the name of dikasts, for the purpose of dealing with the civil and criminal business of the city which came before the courts of law. These 6000 dikasts were divided into what we should call ten juries of 500 each, the remaining 1000 might be reserved for unavoidable vacancies. These ten juries had to hear and determine during the year such complaints and breaches of law as were brought for trial. They were chosen by lot, and they were sworn as our juries are. Which of the ten should be taken on any particular occasion was decided by lot, so that no one knew beforehand which dikastery would try any special case. It is not certain of what exact number each dikastery actually consisted, but it is known they were always numerous. A jury with us must consist of twelve; under the Athenian system 500 were told off to form a jury, though less than 500 might try cases. None of the dikasts could know in what causes they would be employed, so that no one could tamper with them beforehand. They were in reality nothing but jury trials applied, on a scale broad, systematic, unaided, and uncontrolled, and they exhibit in exaggerated proportions both the excellence and the defects of the jury system as compared with decisions by trained and professional judges. The dikasts judged of the law as well as of the fact; the laws were not numerous, and were expressed in few, and for the most part familiar, words. Each dikastery construed the law for itself without being bound by decisions which had been given previously. This method of procedure was, no doubt, adopted to protect the citizens against the domination of the rich and powerful. Good or bad, it was applicable to all, and Socrates fell under its operation. The dikast must be considered to represent the average man of the time and neighbourhood, exempt, indeed, from pecuniary corruption or personal fear, deciding according to what he thinks justice or to some genuine feeling of equity, mercy, religion, or patriotism which, in reference to the case before him, he thinks as good as justice, but not exempt from sympathies, antipathies, prejudices, all of which act the more powerfully because there is often no consciousness of their presence, and because they even appear essential to his ideas of plain and straightforward good sense. We need only look to our own State trials, or to trials which have taken place in times of political excitement, to notice how widely and wildly juries have given verdicts, and we may safely say that 500 Athenian dikasts would be as likely to return a fair and reasonable verdict, according to their means of judging, as an English jury. The actual number of dikasts who tried Socrates is said to have been 501 (281 against 220).

The accusers of Socrates had to prove their indictment against him. They addressed the dikasts, and produced such evidence as they thought necessary; and we must bear in mind that the sort of offence with which he was charged is not difficult to establish, and is difficult to disprove. We see that Euthyphro thought that the genius or dæmon by which Socrates professed to be guided would be classed by the Athenians with the gods. In the Acts of the Apostles, the Athenians say of St Paul, "he seemeth to be a setter forth of strange gods." In the original the word translated gods is δαιμονιων; so that if this word dæmon was at Athens connected with the directing voice which Socrates so often referred to, the Athenians might not unfairly do what our translators have done—interpreted it by the word "gods." We don't know what Socrates meant by the word, and the Athenians did not know. Xenophon makes use of it in connection with Socrates. Was it a person, or what was it? What did the Athenians think of it? For that is the criterion to which we must bring it; and if the language of Socrates was ambiguous and left it doubtful what was meant, the more religious of the dikasts would be apt to put a bad construction upon his language. His duty as an Athenian citizen, according to the notions prevailing there and then, was to conform to the religious customs of his countrymen, and all his searching and probing of men's minds would tend to create suspicion, and his talk about the dæmon or voice which directed him would puzzle his audience still more, and add to the suspicion with which he was regarded. Existences are divided into persons and things. Into which of these categories was this admonisher of Socrates to be placed ? His accusers could, without doubt, put their case in such a way that their charge would seem to be made out; it was precisely the ordinary conduct of Socrates which was alleged against him. The bulk of the Athenians were content with their religion. Socrates had, day by day for twenty years, tried to make them dissatisfied with themselves in connection with subjects which had relation to their gods. He had perplexed and vexed them ; he had convicted them of ignorance, and he had wounded their self-love. He had interrogated them respecting justice and piety and devotion; and he had shown them how hollow their notions were respecting them, and they were naturally irritated. Socrates very well knew that they disliked him on account of his conduct, but he was not to be turned from his purpose, and whether they would hear or whether they would forbear, as the old Hebrew prophet says, he would persevere.

We see, then, that the accusers of Socrates might

not have a difficult task in making out their accusation. They were the plaintiffs; they made their speeches and produced their evidence, and then Socrates had to reply. His reply is contained in that dialogue of Plato called "The Apology." We do not know how much of it was actually spoken by Socrates, but we may be sure that it represents the substance and spirit of what he said. Xenophon tells us that Socrates might have been acquitted if in any moderate degree he would have conciliated the favour of the dikasts; but his speech throughout breathes a spirit of defiance. He stood before his judges with a lofty sense of conscious rectitude; he appealed from the decision of a tribunal necessarily composed of men who were in different degrees prejudiced against him to that higher judicature which sprang from his own reason and conscience; moreover, he was not afraid to face the consequence of his actions. It was not an uncommon thing for a man who was accused before the dikasts to bring his wife and children into court, and through them to appeal to the compassion of his judges. Socrates would do nothing of the kind. He knew that his course of life had laid him open to the charges made against him; he knew that his freedom of speech had offended the Athenians; he knew that, in fact, there was a great gulf between him and them;

not that he disowned or denied his country's gods, but he sought to awaken and arouse some new thought among his countrymen, and to translate the forms and shams which made up much of their religion into some intelligent and living reality. Socrates knew that his purpose had been good and noble, but he knew also that it had been misunderstood and misrepresented, and he was prepared to pay the penalty. He had for a long series of years attempted to teach the Athenians in an indirect but searching manner; he was convinced that in no other way could he get a hearing, and so he persevered. The proof of his judgment and his skill, and of the general fairness and toleration of the Athenians, is that he was allowed to exercise his self-imposed and irritating vocation for so many years. We have only to recollect what sharp and sudden commotions occurred when the special religious feelings of Jews and Asiatics were assailed in order to measure the intellectual difference between the one set of people and the other. One or two extracts may be made from the defence of Socrates. He says: "The young men who follow me about, who are the sons of wealthy persons and with much leisure, by nature delight in hearing men cross-questioned; and they often imitate me among themselves. Then they try their hand at cross-questioning other people, and I imagine they find a great abundance of men who think that they know a great deal when, in truth, they know little or nothing. And then the persons who are cross-questioned are angry with me instead of with themselves, and say, Socrates is an abominable fellow who corrupts the young. And when they were asked, Why, what does he do? what does he teach? they have nothing to say. But not to seem at a loss, they repeat the stock charges against all philosophers, and say, that he investigates things in the air and under the earth, and that he teaches people to disbelieve in the gods, and to make the worst appear the better reason. And so they have filled your ears with their fierce slanders for a long time, for they are zealous and fierce and numerous. They are well disciplined, too, and plausible in speech. On these grounds Melêtus and Anytus and Lykon have attacked me. Melêtus is angry with me for the poets, Anytus for the artisans and public men, and Lykon for the orators. And I should be surprised if I were able in so short a time to remove this prejudice of yours which has grown so great." We see from this the extent of the ill-feeling which existed against Socrates. He knew it, and he seems to admit that it was natural for the Athenians in their then state of knowledge to dislike and oppose his teaching. Further on he says: "If you were to say to me, 'Socrates, this time we will let you go on condition that you cease from carrying on this search and from philosophy. If you are found doing this again you shall die '—I say, if you offered to let me go on these grounds I should reply: 'Athenians, I hold you in the highest regard and love, but I will obey the god rather than you; and as long as I have breath and power I will not cease from philosophy and from exhorting you and setting forth the truth to any of you whom I meet, saying as I am wont: "My excellent friend, you are a citizen of Athens, a city very great and very famous for wisdom and power of mind; are you not ashamed of caring so much for the making of money and for reputation and honour? Will you not spend thought or care on wisdom and truth and perfecting your soul?' And if he dispute my words, and say that he does care for these things, I shall not forthwith release him and go away; I shall question him and cross-examine him; and if I think that he has not virtue, though he says that he has, I shall reproach him for setting the lowest value on the most important things and the highest value on the most worthless." He winds up in this way: "I do not think it right to entreat the judge nor to gain acquittal by entreaties: he should be convinced by argument. He does not sit to make a present of justice, but to give judgment; and he has sworn to judge according to law, and not to favour a man whom he likes. And so we ought not to ask you to forswear yourselves; and you ought not to allow us to do so, for then neither of us would be acting righteously. Therefore, Athenians, do not require me to do these things, for I hold them to be neither good nor just nor holy, more especially now when Melêtus is indicting me for impiety. To you, therefore and to God, I commit my cause, to be determined by you as is best for you and me."

The dikasts, having heard the accusation and the defence, gave their votes. For acquitting Socrates there were 220: he was condemned by 281, so that the majority against him was 61. His accusers were then asked what punishment they proposed, and Melêtus replied "Death." Socrates was then at liberty to propose a lighter penalty, and he said: "There are many reasons, O men of Athens, why I am not grieved at the vote of condemnation. I expected this, and am only surprised that the votes are so nearly equal, for I thought the majority against me would have been larger. And so he proposes death as the penalty. And what shall I propose on my part, O men of Athens? Clearly that which is my due. And what is that which I ought to pay or to receive? What shall be done to the man who has never had the wit to be idle during his whole life, who has been careless of what the many care about—wealth and family interests and military offices, and speaking in the Assembly and magistracies and plots and parties? What shall be done to such an one? Doubtless some good thing, if he has his reward: and the good should be of a kind suitable to him. What would be a reward suitable to a poor man who is your benefactor, and who desires leisure that he may instruct you? Perhaps you may think I am braving you in saying this, as in what I said before about the tears and prayers; but this is not so. I speak rather because I am convinced that I never intentionally wronged anyone. I will not say of myself that I deserve any evil, or propose any penalty. Why should I? Because I am afraid of the penalty of death which Melêtus proposes? When I do not know whether death is a good or an evil, why should I propose a penalty which would certainly be an evil? He then mentions imprisonment or banishment, which, he says, are real evils, and he will not propose them; and as to a fine, he asserts that he has no money, but that perhaps his friends might be security for a small sum. In the end, as he proposes no mitigation of the penalty, which is even possible, the sentence of death is passed. On this part of the subject, Dr Thirlwall, late Bishop of St David's, says: "It seems that the law required judgment to be passed according to the proposal either of the prosecutor or the defendant."

Having named Dr Thirlwall, I will make another extract from his work, as it throws light on the subject, and raises a question which we are bound to discuss. He says: "The time in which Socrates was brought to trial was one in which great zeal was professed, and some was undoubtedly felt, for the revival of the ancient institutions, civil and religious, under which Athens had attained her past greatness; and it was to be expected that all who traced the public calamities to the neglect of the old laws and usages should consider Socrates a dangerous person." This is an admission which is made by all the writers I am acquainted with. That Athenian life and thought were in a state of transition everyone is compelled to admit, and it is important, coming from Dr Thirlwall; and we are bound to follow it up by the further consideration that a fermentation of civil and religious ideas, and a feeling that false ones were gaining the ascendency and were tending to national calamity, was a state of mind unfavourable to what may be called judicial fairness. The Athenians thought, as Dr Thirlwall allows, that certain public calamities were attributable to the decay and the neglect of old laws and usages, and if they believed that the teaching of Socrates promoted this decay and neglect, then it was a respectable feeling which led them to dislike and to oppose him. His notions and theirs were at variance. They believed him to be wrong; he believed them to be so. He was much wiser than they were; but where is the people who are willing to admit this under such circumstances? On their side they had the prescription of the past, the persuasion that their country had grown great by means and instrumentalities which were, in their opinion, crumbling in pieces, and which it seemed to them Socrates was helping to undermine, and which it is probable he was really doing. Dr Thirlwall has a very elaborate note in reply to German criticism on the case of Socrates, and he concludes in these words: "There never was a case in which murder was more clearly committed under the forms of legal procedure than in the trial of Socrates. Judicial murders more atrocious in their circumstances may have been perpetrated by the Roman Senate under the Emperors, by the Holy Office, and by the Revolutionary Tribunal under the Reign of Terror." Dr Thirlwall was a man of great learning and of sound judgment, whose "Life and Letters"—most interesting and valuable—have just been published; but this dictum of his appears to me, though it seems rash to say it, a hasty and inconsiderate one. He had just before said in respect of religious opinion in Athens: "There was no canon, no book by which a doctrine could be tried; no living authority to which appeal could be made for the decision of religious controversies. Beyond the bare fact of the existence of the beings who were objects of public worship, there was hardly a circumstance in their history which had not been related in many different ways; and there was no form of the legend which had more or less claim to be received than another. So that if Socrates rejected every version of the fable which appeared to him to have an immoral tendency, he was only exercising a right which could not be legally disputed, and was taking no greater liberty than had been used by many others without any scandal." This argument is in every way, as it seems to me, a fallacious one. If there was an offence concerning religious belief and practice, dealt with as impiety by Athenian law, and if there existed no canon or book by which religious opinions were to be tested, by what means were the dikasts to ascertain when the offence was committed, and how are they to be blamed if, in a confessedly undefinable offence which they were bound to try, they came to a conclusion in accordance with those views and beliefs which, however imperfectly understood by them, were almost universally acknowledged? To know whether a man has committed an offence, it is absolutely needful that the offence should be defined. Legal murder is not killing a man, but killing him under defined circumstances and with particular intentions; and impiety, if not defined, is just what each man thinks it to be, and no two men may exactly agree about it; who then is to blame—the law or the jury? Besides, no one knew better than the Bishop that the meaning of such words as these was just the main controversy between Socrates and his hearers. It is the very essence of the discussion between him and Euthyphro. "What," he asks, "is impiety?" Euthyphro answers, but his answers fail when tested. It was precisely this want of critical faculty which Socrates was for ever denouncing. The Bishop admits that there was no canon or book by which religious opinions were to be tested, and he blames the Athenian dikasts because they could not supply the deficiency. He had surely forgotten the causes which had come before our own Ecclesiastical Courts of late years, and which his letters prove he had considered so deeply; and how the keenest intellects of a trained legal profession had been unable to agree upon the meaning of documents which they had to construe. He must have forgotten how conflicting are the interpretations which our Judges and Law Courts put upon the words of the same Act of Parliament; and yet he impugns the honesty of the Athenian dikasts because, being sworn without the aid of any canon or book to determine whether certain words and acts amounted to impiety and to the disparagement of their gods, they came to a conclusion which is not acceptable to an English Bishop of the nineteenth century who has access to books and commentaries which they never heard of, and which, in fact, did not exist. The Bishop acknowledges that the biographies of these fabulous divinities were in a most chaotic condition. Their genealogies were utterly out of joint, their actions apocryphal, contradictory, and absurd. Put into the Bishop's critical crucible, no doubt these inconsistencies and extravagances emerge; but then he forgets to tell us that this apparatus of criticism the dikasts did not possess, and that they had to decide according to that version of the history in which they had been instructed and which had fallen in their way. The Bishop knew very well, when writing his history in a secluded parish in Yorkshire, that if he had asked his Sunday congregation a few plain questions upon high matters of theology, they would not have given very intelligent answers, though they had been taught their catechism and their creed, and for years had had the advantage of his own, no doubt, most instructive teaching. The Athenian dikasts lacked this special light and guidance; they had as hard a question to solve; and when we are measuring their merits and demerits, we must compare them not with the profoundest scholar and divine of this century, but with the average people we meet with, and we must give them the benefit of any doubt that we may feel. Further, Dr Thirlwall quite overlooks the fact that the right of discussing what he calls these fables might be exercised by a writer of poetry or of philosophy without shocking the sentiments of the populace; but Socrates took a course which brought him into active, ceaseless, and personal conflict with every man upon whom he could fasten his interrogatories. Once more, Dr Thirlwall alleges "the difficulty which most persons in modern times have felt in reconciling the pure and lofty ideas which Socrates appears to have formed of the Divine nature with a belief in the doctrines or fables of the Greek polytheism." Again, Dr Thirlwall does not notice the circumstance that what to him is now fable, to an Athenian was once fact; and if he is astonished that Socrates, with pure and lofty ideas, believed what are now reckoned absurd fables, had he no excuse or toleration for the Athenian dikast, who had not reached the pure and lofty ideal of Socrates, but only that meaner level of those absurd fables, which Socrates, while professedly believing, handled in such way that the simple Athenian dikast was unable to reconcile with honest belief and sincerity? Dr Thirlwall was puzzled that Socrates held what appeared to him to be contradictory and antagonistic beliefs. To the Athenian dikast it was equally inconceivable that Socrates really believed the common creed, while speaking and acting as he did; he could not make these two things fit, as Dr Thirlwall could not make the others fit. Let us do justice to the Athenian dikast and to the Athenian people, remembering that the events we are considering happened something like 500 years before the Christian era. It is clear that there existed at Athens in the time of Socrates some law against what was then reckoned impiety; some legal condemnation of the conduct which disregarded or outraged the general feeling respecting the gods and their worship. There are such laws in England now. That which Englishmen hold sacred the law protects, and punishes those who violate it. What is such a violation, as the law intends to forbid, may be difficult to determine, and honest men may easily disagree about it; and whatever the particular acts might be which Athenian law meant to put down might be very dubious and debatable; but a jury must give a verdict, and our own law and practice, until lately, famished the jury and left them without fire and light until they agreed. Something at Athens, as well as in England, was and is offensive to the religious feelings of the people, and, for this reason, liable to legal penalty. It is curious to notice how the strong sense of a Roman proconsul broke through this kind of accusation; and, moreover, what a striking contrast there is between the Jew and the Greek in the presence of that which contradicted his custom and belief. We are told in the Acts of the Apostles that the Jews made insurrection with one accord against Paul, and brought him to the judgment seat, because, as they said, he "persuadeth men to worship God contrary to the law." Substantially the same charge as that brought against Socrates, and, moreover, it was at the Greek city of Corinth that this happened, and it produced an instant outburst of insurrection by the Jews. Before Paul had time to make any defence the Roman proconsul Gallio said: "If it were a matter of wrong or wicked lewdness, O Jews, reason would that I should bear with you; but if it be a question of words and names and of your law, look ye to it; for I will be no judge of such." This Roman proconsul had a clear perception of the province of government. But the other idea was, and had been, far more prevalent—the idea that government should not only restrain bad and unjust acts, but should control and punish speculative opinions and what it might consider the misuse of Gallio's "words and names." We should have to travel very far back to find the origin of this notion. But we are all familiar with the history of Nebuchadnezzar, which was not of much earlier date than that of Socrates. There was no circumlocution or beating about the bush with this ruler of Babylon. He decreed in the most peremptory style that everybody was to worship as he wished, on pain of being burned to death. Athens was much more moderate than this oriental monarch ; nevertheless, his example was followed everywhere, with more or less stringency, not amongst Pagans only of that era, but amongst Christians of a much later one. In the 4th century of our era, Theodosius the Great made certain religious acts of his heathen subjects punishable as high treason with death, and for other acts of the same sort he inflicted ruinous fines and forfeitures. Gibbon tells us that he repeatedly enforced these persecuting decrees with the applause of a large portion of his subjects. The latest English historian of these times—a most painstaking, pictorial, and impartial writer, Mr Hodgkin —says : " For some generations, with quiet, earnest deliberateness, the whole power of the Emperors was employed in making all Christians think alike, and in preventing non-Christians thinking at all."* The Theodosian code remains to testify to the severity of its enactments, and is a sort of landmark in the region we are traversing ; and for many centuries such legislation was in the ascendant. Two or three examples from the many which might be selected will be enough for our purpose.

In the 16th century of grace, Giordano Bruno, a man of literary eminence and of blameless life, was burned at Rome on account of his religious opinions, one of the official spectators of the burning exclaim-

* Italy and her Invaders.

ing, "Such is the way in which we at Rome deal with impious men," impiety being exactly the offence with which Socrates was charged. In the same century, Michael Servetus, a man of unimpeachable character, and an author of distinction, was burned at Geneva because his writings were judged to be heretical. These men, and a host of others who might be named, were put to death, not for any crime which they committed, but because, like Socrates, they held opinions and propagated them, which were condemned by their contemporaries. History could furnish us with a long catalogue of such cases. I will select one more from our own annals. Whoever has been to Oxford and taken note of its beauties will have observed in one of the streets a monument, erected some few years ago to commemorate the public burning, near the spot where it stands, of three English Bishops—Latimer, Ridley, and Cranmer. There was no crime proved against these men; they were put to death because, like Socrates, they diverged from the then dominant religion. Our apology for 'the Athenian dikast is that he believed Socrates to be a heretic; and it is exactly this offence which was charged against those three Bishops, and for which they suffered. Socrates, as a man and a citizen, could fearlessly appeal to his judges and say : "I never intentionally wronged anyone," and not less truly could these three Bishops make the same challenge; as citizens they were in all respects the equals, it may be the superiors, of Socrates.

Shakespeare, who lived not many years after Cranmer, knew his history and the traditions connected with it, and he puts into his mouth these words, addressed to the Council:—

> My good lords, hitherto, in all the progress
> Both of my life and office, I have laboured,
> And with no little study, that my teaching
> And the strong course of my authority
> Might go one way and safely; and the end
> Was ever to do well; nor is there living—
> I speak it with a single heart, my lords—
> A man that more detests, more stirs against
> Both in his private conscience and his place,
> Defacers of the public peace, than I do.
> Pray Heaven, the King may never find a heart
> With less allegiance in it. Men that make
> Envy and crooked malice nourishment
> Dare bite the best. I do beseech your lordships
> That in this case of justice, my accusers,
> Be what they will, may stand forth face to face
> And freely urge against me.

It is not pertinent to inquire into the particular opinions and beliefs which have brought men into peril and to death. We stand beside the culprit and his accusers, and it is a charge of impiety which is brought against him; and on such a charge it was that Socrates was arraigned. The impiety of one age is not in its form that of another; the divinities may be different, but so far as the offender is concerned, he has always contravened the public estimate of them, and for this he is condemned.

We are not concerned with this general question, except so far as it is applicable to Athens. We have a right to compare her case with that of others, and it is needful to revive these old stories in order that we may relieve Athens of some odium, if we find that other States were not only as harsh as she was, but that, having better opportunities and wiser teaching, were even more unrelenting and harder of heart. Let us carry our comparison to the bitter end, and for this purpose I quote from Tennyson's "Queen Mary" the account of the burning of Cranmer.

Enter *Peters*.

Peters, my gentleman, an honest Catholic,
Who follow'd with the crowd to Cranmer's fire.
One that would neither misreport nor lie,
Not to gain paradise ; no, nor if the Pope
Charged him to do it—he is white as death.
Peters, how pale you look ! you bring the smoke
Of Cranmer's burning with you.

Peters.
                            Twice or thrice
The smoke of Cranmer's burning wrapt me round.

Howard.

Peters, you know me Catholic, but English.
Did he die bravely ? Tell me that, or leave
All else untold.

                    Peters.
                My lord, he died most bravely.
                    Howard.
Then tell me all.
                    Paget.
                Ay, Master Peters, tell us.
                    Peters.
You saw him how he passed among the crowd ;
And ever as he walk'd the Spanish friars
Still plied him with entreaty and reproach :
But Cranmer, as the helmsman at the helm
Steers, ever looking to the happy haven
Where he shall rest at night, moved to his death ;
And I could see that many silent hands
Came from the crowd and met his own ; and thus,
When we had come where Ridley burnt with Latimer,
He, with a cheerful smile, as one whose mind
Is all made up, in haste put off the rags
They had mock'd his misery with, and all in white,
His long white beard, which he had never shaven
Since Henry's death, down-sweeping to the chain,
Wherewith they bound him to the stake, he stood,
More like an ancient father of the Church,
Than heretic of these times ; and still the friars
Plied him, but Cranmer only shook his head,
Or answer'd them in smiling negatives ;
Whereat Lord Williams gave a sudden cry :—
"Make short ! make short ! " and so they lit the wood,
Then Cranmer lifted his left hand to heaven,
And thrust his right into the bitter flame ;
And crying, in his deep voice, more than once,
"This hath offended—this unworthy hand ! "
So held it till it all was burned, before
The flame had reached his body ; I stood near—

Mark'd him—he never uttered moan of pain ;
He never stirr'd or writhed, but, like a statue,
Unmoving in the greatness of the flame,
Gave up the ghost ; and so past martyr-like—
Martyr I may not call him—past—but whither ?

" Look on that picture and on this."

I quote again from " Social Life in Greece," by the Rev. Professor Mahaffy.

There is a very different point suggested by the life of Socrates, which proves the refined culture of the Athenians from another side. It is an universal contrast between civilised and semi-civilised societies (not to speak of barbarians), that the penalty of death, when legally incurred, is in the former carried out without cruelty and torture, whereas in the latter the victim of the law is farther punished by insults and by artificial pains. The punishments devised by kings and barons in the middle ages, the hideous torments devised by the Church for the bodies of those whose souls were doomed to even worse for ever and ever—these cases will occur to any reader from the history of semi-civilised nations. It will not perhaps strike him that our own country was hardly better even in the present century, and that the formula now uttered by the judge in sentencing to death suggests by its very wording horrible cruelties threatened almost within the memory of living men. ' That you be hanged by the neck, *till you are dead*,' points to the form uttered in the courts of Dublin within this century, though not then literally carried out. It ran thus : ' It is therefore ordered by the Court that they and each of them be taken from the bar of the Court where they now stand, to the place from whence they came—the gaol : that their irons be there stricken off, that they be from thence carried to the common place of execution, the gallows ; and that they and each of them be hanged by the neck, *but not until they be dead, for whilst they are yet alive they are to be taken down, their entrails are to be taken out of their body, and whilst they are yet alive they are to be burned before their faces;* their heads are then to be respectively cut off; their bodies to be respectively divided into four quarters; and their respective heads and bodies to be at His Majesty's disposal.'

Let us now compare these formulæ, used by the most cultivated and humane European nation in the nineteenth century, with the enactments of the Athenian democracy four hundred years before Christ. In the first place, there was no penalty permitted severer than a quiet and painless death. There were no antecedent insults and cruelties, no aggravations, no exhibitions before a heartless and ribald mob. In the next place, care had been taken to ascertain the most easy and gentle death, as Xenophon distinctly implies (*Apol. Socr.* § 7), and for this reason death by poisoning with hemlock was introduced—at what exact period, we cannot say. Here, again, the Athenians were in advance even of the present day, when death by hanging, in the hands of ignorant and careless officials, is often a slow death, and a death of torture. But all this is to my mind far less significant than the *manner* of Athenian executions, as compared with those even of our day. We have fortunately in Plato's "Phædo" a detailed account of this scene, which, however imaginary as to the conversations introduced, must have lost all its dramatic propriety and force to Plato's contemporaries, had not the details been reproduced from life with faithful accuracy.

There, is, I think, in all Greek literature no scene which ought to make us more ashamed of our boasted Christian culture. The condemned, on the day of execution, was freed from his chains, and allowed to have his family and friends present in his cell, as they had already been during the nights of his imprisonment.

The condemned then was left with his family and friends, to make his arrangements and bequests, to give his last directions, to comfort and to be comforted by those dearest to him. When the hour of death approached, the gaoler came in, and left the cup of poison with the victim, giving him directions how to take it, and merely adding that it must be done before a certain hour. He then retired and left the prisoner in his last moments to the care of his friends. They sat about him as life gradually ebbed away, and closed his eyes in peace.

Compare all this humane and kindly feeling with the gauntness and horror of our modern executions, as detailed to us with morbid satisfaction by our daily newspapers. The whole scene in Socrates' prison is, as I said, the greatest proof I know in Greek literature of a culture exceeding in refinement and humanity that of our own day.

Once more, in the recent work, "Don John of Austria," by the late Sir William Stirling-Maxwell, there is a description of a Spanish *auto-da-fé*, which it is not unfair to contrast with the proceedings at Athens, in the case of Socrates:—

"In Valladolid in 1559, when the flowers of May bloomed in the gardens of the Pisuerga, the sky was darkened by the smoke which went up from the human sacrifices of the Inquisition. The past year had been marked by a movement towards religious reform, the first and the last that history has yet had to record in Spain. Compared with the mighty revolution of the north, so fruitful of great men and great events, the Spanish movement was feeble in its origin, unfortunate in its instruments, and worthless in its results. It was neither called for by the political necessities of the nation, nor supported by its sympathy. Its chiefs were a few clergymen, chosen long before by Charles V. for their learning and worth, and employed by him, or by his son, to watch the progress of heresy in the Netherlands and Germany, and to guard from contamination the Spaniards brought by civil or military service within reach of the pestilence. These divines soon saw that the victories of reform from without, were to be met only by reform from within, begun and carried on by the Church itself. . . . The question whether all or any of their doctrines were orthodox or heretical, affords a wide field for argument to those who 'think the shadowy frontier between heresy and orthodoxy worth defining. But there is no reason for believing that their aims were schismatic, or that they were less the true and loving children of Mother Church than those who condemned and massacred them as apostates."

The execution is thus described—"Fifteen were sentences of death, and were immediately carried into execution. The Princess-Regent of Spain and the noble knights and dames of Castille looked on as the flames crept and leaped round the tortured limbs of men who had been their familiar friends and spiritual advisers, of fair and delicate women dragged from splendid homes or from the solitude of the cloister to die for opinions of which neither they nor their persecutors have been able to give any intelligible account."

This transaction has no parallel in the criminal proceedings of pagan Athens.

We have to consider, in relation to all these various acts, that at the times of which we have been speaking, it was an offence, a crime, to disbelieve and to dispute the publicly-approved religion; and we may fairly ask which State, upon the whole, was mildest and most tolerant in its method of punishing, and we may at least award to the State so distinguished the palm of humanity. Let us now follow Socrates into his prison. The story of his last hours is to be found in Plato's dialogue, "Phædo," and it is introduced in this manner: After an interval of some months or years, and at Phlius, a town of Sicyon, Echecrates and some of his friends meet Phædo and ask him to narrate to them the circumstances of the death of Socrates, as the minutest particulars of the event are interesting to distant friends. Thereupon Phædo commences the narrative, from which I can only select a few passages. Echecrates asks Phædo:—

Were you yourself, Phædo, in the prison with Socrates on the day when he drank the poison?
Ph. Yes, Echecrates, I was.
Ech. I wish you would tell me about his death. What did he say in his last hours? We were told that he died by taking poison, but no one knew anything more; for none of us ever go to Athens now, and Athenians do not come here, so that we have had no account of what happened.
Ph. Did you not hear of the proceedings of the trial?
Ech. Yes; some one told us about the trial; and we could not understand why, having been condemned, he was put to death, not at the time, but long afterwards. What was the reason of this?
Ph. An accident, Echecrates. The reason was that the stern of the ship which the Athenians sent to Delos happened to have been crowned on the day before he was tried.
Ech. What is this ship?

Ph. This is the ship in which, as the Athenians say, Theseus went to Crete when he took with him the fourteen youths, and was the saviour of them and of himself. And they were said to have vowed to Apollo at the time that if they were saved they would make an annual pilgrimage to Delos. Now this custom still continues, and the whole period of the voyage to and from Delos, beginning when the Priest of Apollo crowns the stern of the ship, is a holy season, during which the city is not allowed to be polluted by public executions. The ship was crowned on the day before the trial, and this was the reason why Socrates lay in prison and was not put to death till long after he was condemned.

Ech. What was the manner of his death, Phædo? What was said or done? and which of his friends had he with him? or were they not allowed by the authorities to be present? and did he die alone?

Ph. No; there were several of his friends with him.

Ech. If you have nothing to do, I wish you would tell me what passed as exactly as you can.

Ph. I have nothing to do, and I will gratify your wish; for to me, too, there is no greater pleasure than to have Socrates brought to my recollection, whether I speak myself or hear another speak of him.

Ech. You will have listeners who are of the same mind with you, and I hope you will be as exact as you can.

Ph. I remember the strange feeling that came over me at being with him, for I could hardly believe I was present at the death of a friend, and therefore I did not pity him, Echecrates; his mien and his language were so noble and fearless in the hour of death that to me he appeared blessed. I thought that in going to the other world he would not be without a divine call, and that he would be happy, if any man ever was, when he arrived there, and therefore I did not pity him, as might seem natural at such a time. But neither could I feel the pleasure which I usually felt in philosophical discourse (for philosophy was the theme of which we spoke). I was pleased, and I was also pained, because I knew that he was soon to die, and this strange feeling was shared by us all; we were laughing and weeping by turns, especially the excitable Appolodorus. You know the sort of man.

Ech. Yes.

Ph. He was quite overcome, and I myself, and all of us were greatly moved.

Ech. Who were present?

Ph. Of native Athenians there were, besides Appolodorus, Critobulus and his father Crito, Hermogenes, Epigenes, Æschines, and Antisthenes; likewise Ctesippus, Menexenus, and some others; but Plato, if am not mistaken, was ill.

Ech. Were there any strangers?

Ph. Yes, there were; Simmias the Theban, and Cebes, Phædondes, Euclid, and Terpsion, who came from Megara.

Ech. And was Aristippus there and Cleombrotus?

Ph. No, they were said to be in Ægina.

Ech. Anyone else?

Ph. I think these were about all.

Ech. And what was the discourse of which you spoke?

Ph. I will begin at the beginning and endeavour to repeat the entire conversation. You must understand that we had been previously in the habit of assembling early in the morning at the court in which the trial was held, and which is not far from the prison. There we remained talking with one another until the opening of the prison doors (for they were opened very early), and then went in and passed the day with Socrates. On the last morning the meeting was earlier than usual. This was owing to our having heard on the previous evening that the sacred ship had arrived from Delos, and therefore we agreed to meet very early at the accustomed place. On our going to the prison, the gaoler who answered the door, instead of admitting us, came out and bade us wait and he would call us, "for the eleven," he said, "are now with Socrates, they are taking off his chains and giving orders that he is to die today." He soon returned and said that we might come in. On entering we found Socrates just released frrom chains, and Xanthippe, whom you know, sitting by him, and holding his child in her arms. When she saw us she uttered a cry and said, as women will : "O, Socrates, this is the last time that either you will converse with your friends or they with you." Socrates turned to Crito and said : "Crito, let some one take her home." Some of Crito's people accordingly led her away crying out and beating herself. And when she was gone, Socrates, sitting on the couch, began to bend and rub his leg, saying, as he rubbed : "How singular is the thing called pleasure, and how curiously related to pain, which might be thought to be the opposite of it; for they never come to a man together, and yet he who pursues either of them is generally compelled to take the other." He pursues this topic, and afterwards says : "I am quite ready to acknowledge that I ought to be grieved at death, if I were not persuaded that I am going to other gods who are wise and good (of this I am as certain as I can be of anything of the sort), and to men departed (though I am not so certain of this) who are better than those whom I leave behind ; and, therefore, I do not grieve as I might have done, for I have good hope that there is yet something remaining for the dead, and, as has been said of old, some far better thing for the good than for the evil." Crito then says : "The attendant who is to give you the poison has been telling me that you are not to talk much, and he wants me to let you know this; for that by talking, heat is increased, and this interferes with the action of the poison. Those who excite themselves are sometimes obliged to drink the poison two or three times." "Then," said Socrates, "let him mind his business and be prepared to give the poison two or three times, if necessary; that is all." "I was almost certain you would say that," replied Crito; "but I was obliged to satisfy him." "Never mind him," he said.

Then follows a lengthened discussion upon the immortality of the soul, of which it is not possible to give even a sketch, and which is probably regarded by modern readers as more fanciful than substantial. It is, no doubt, the argument of Plato more than of Socrates; but the dramatic fitness of the discussion under the circumstances must be at once recognised; and the attitude of Socrates, his serenity, his courage, his cheerfulness, his moral earnestness, must be regarded as a true portraiture of his conduct during the last hours of his life. Like the spectators at the time, we cannot pity Socrates; his mien and his language are so noble and fearless. He is the same as he ever was, but milder and gentler. Perhaps the extreme elevation of Socrates above his own situation, and the ordinary interests of life, create in the mind an impression stronger than could be derived from arguments that such an one, in his own language, has in him "a principle that does not admit of death." Having in the course of the discussion described what may be the future destiny of the soul, he concludes in this way:—

"I don't mean to affirm that the description I have given of the soul and her mansions is exactly true, a man of sense would hardly say that; but I do say that, inasmuch as the soul is shown to be immortal, we may venture to think, not improperly or unworthily, that something of the kind is true. Wherefore, I say, let the man be of good cheer who has adorned the soul in her proper jewels, which are temperance and justice, and courage and nobility and worth, and arrayed in these *she* is ready to go on her journey to the world below when her time comes." Then turning to us he said : " You and all other men will depart at some time or other; to *me*, already, as the tragic poet would say, 'the voice of fate calls; for soon I must drink the poison."

Phædo continues the narrative :—

" When he had done speaking, Crito said, 'And have you any commands for us, Socrates ; anything to say about your children, or any other matter on which we can serve you?' 'Nothing particular,' he said, 'only, as I have always told you, I would have you look to yourselves ; that is a service you may always be doing to me and mine as well as yourselves.' When he had spoken these words he arose and went into the bath chamber with Crito, who bade us wait, and we waited, talking and thinking of the subject of discourse, and also of the greatness of our sorrow. He was like a father of whom we were being bereaved, and we were about to pass the rest of our lives as orphans. When he had taken the bath his children were brought to him (he had two young sons and an elder one), and the women of his family also came, and he talked to them and gave them a few directions in the presence of Crito, and he then dismissed them and returned to us.

" Now the hour of sunset was near—the hour when the hemlock was to be drunk. He sat down with us again after the bath, but not much was said. Soon the gaoler, who was the servant of the eleven, entered and stood by him, saying, 'To you, Socrates, whom I know to be the noblest and gentlest and best of all who ever came to this place, I will not impute the angry feelings of other men who rage and swear at me when, in obedience to the authorities I bid them drink the poison; indeed, I am sure that you will not be angry with me, for others, as you are aware, and not I, are the guilty cause. And so, fare you well, and try to bear lightly what must needs be. You know my errand.' Then bursting into tears he turned away and went out. Socrates looked at him and said, 'I return your good wishes and will do as you bid.' Then turning to us he said, 'How kindly the man is! Since I have been in prison he has always been coming to see me, and at times he would talk to me and was as good as he could be to me; and now, see how generously he sorrows for me. But we must do as he says, Crito; let the cup be brought, if the poison is prepared, and if not, let the attendant prepare some.' 'Yet,' said Crito, '*the sun is still upon the hill tops*, and many a one has taken the draught late, and after the announcement has been made to him, he has eaten and drunk, and indulged in other such delights; do not hasten, *there is still time; the sun yet lingers*.' 'Yes, Crito,' said Socrates, 'the people of whom you speak were right in doing thus, because they thought they would gain by the delay; but I am right in not doing so, for I do not think I should gain anything by drinking the poison a little later. I should be sparing and saving a life which is already gone. I could only smile at myself for this. Please, then, do as I say, and do not refuse me.'

"Crito when he heard this made a sign to the servant, and the servant went in and remained for some time, and then returned with the gaoler carrying the cup of poison. Socrates said: 'You, my good friend, who are experienced in these matters, shall give me directions how I am to proceed.' The man replied: 'You have only to walk about

SOCRATES AND THE ATHENIANS. 71

until your legs are heavy, and then to lie down and the poison will act.' At the same time he handed the cup to Socrates, who in the easiest and gentlest manner, without the least fear or change of colour or feature, looking at the man steadfastly, as his manner was, took the cup and said: 'What do you say about making a libation out of this cup to any god? May I or not?' The man answered: 'We only prepare, Socrates, just so much as we deem enough.' 'I understand,' he said; 'yet I may, and must, pray to the gods to prosper my journey from this to that other world. May this, then, which is my prayer be granted to me.' Then holding the cup to his lips quite readily and cheerfully he drank off the poison. And hitherto most of us had been able to control our sorrow; but now when we saw him drinking, and saw, too, that he had finished the draught, we could no longer forbear, and in spite of myself my own tears were flowing fast, so that I covered my face and wept over myself, for certainly I was not weeping over him, but at the thought of my own calamity in having lost such a companion. Nor was I the first, for Crito, when he found himself unable to restrain his tears, had got up and moved away, and I followed, and at that moment Apollodorus, who had been weeping all the time, broke out into a loud cry which made cowards of us all.

"Socrates alone retained his calmness. 'What is this strange outcry?' he said. 'I sent away the women mainly in order that they might not offend in this way, for I have heard that a man should die in peace. Be quiet, then, and patient.' When we heard that, we were ashamed, and refrained our tears, and he walked about until, as he said, his legs began to fail, and then he lay down according to the directions; and the man who gave him the poison now and then looked at his feet and legs, and after awhile he pressed his foot hard, and asked him if he could feel, and he said, 'No;' and then his leg, and so upwards and upwards, and showed us that he was cold and stiff. And he felt them himself, and said: 'When the poison reaches the heart that will be the end.' He was beginning to grow cold about the groin, when he uncovered his face, for he had covered himself up, and said (they were his last words): 'Crito, I owe a cock to Asclepius, will you remember to pay the debt?' 'The debt shall be paid,' said Crito. 'Is there anything else?' There was no answer to the question; but in a minute or so a movement was heard and the attendants uncovered him. His eyes were set, and Crito closed his eyes and his mouth. Such was the end, Echecrates, of our friend, whom I may truly call the wisest and justest and best of all the men whom I have ever known."

This judgment of Phædo regarding Socrates has remained unreversed for more than twenty centuries; and in recent times, a representative man, and one of England's greatest poets, attracted to Athens by her ancient renown, and watching the sun set over the Ægean Sea, felt that this story of Socrates was the one most indelibly associated with the scene, and impressed upon his own imagination, and he commemorated it in the following immortal lines:—

> Slow sinks, more lovely ere his race be run
> Along Morea's hills the setting sun;
> Not, as in Northern climes, obscurely bright,
> But one unclouded blaze of living light!
> O'er the hush'd deep the yellow beam he throws,
> Gilds the green wave, that trembles as it glows.
> On old Ægina's rock, and Idra's isle,
> The god of gladness sheds his parting smile;
> O'er his own regions lingering, loves to shine,

Though there his altars are no more divine.
Descending fast the mountain shadows kiss
Thy glorious gulf, unconquer'd Salamis !
Their azure arches through the long expanse
More deeply purpled meet his mellowing glance,
And tenderest tints, along their summits driven,
Mark his gay course, and own the hues of heaven
Till, darkly shaded from the land and deep,
Behind his Delphian cliff he sinks to sleep.

On such an eve, his palest beam he cast,
When—Athens ! here thy Wisest look'd his last.
How watch'd thy better sons his farewell ray,
That closed their murder'd sage's latest day !
Not yet—not yet—Sol pauses on the hill—
The precious hour of parting lingers still ;
But sad his light to agonising eyes,
And dark the mountain's once delightful dyes :
Gloom o'er the lovely land he seem'd to pour,
The land, where Phœbus never frown'd before ;
But ere he sunk below Cithæron's head,
The cup of woe was quaff'd, the spirit fled ;
The soul of him who scorned to fear or fly—
Who lived and died, as none can live or die !

A LIST OF
KEGAN PAUL, TRENCH & CO.'S PUBLICATIONS.

10.83.

1, *Paternoster Square,*
London.

A LIST OF

KEGAN PAUL, TRENCH & CO.'S PUBLICATIONS.

CONTENTS.

	PAGE		PAGE
GENERAL LITERATURE.	2	POETRY.	30
INTERNATIONAL SCIENTIFIC SERIES	26	WORKS OF FICTION	37
		BOOKS FOR THE YOUNG	38
MILITARY WORKS.	29		

GENERAL LITERATURE.

ADAMSON, H. T., B.D.—The Truth as it is in Jesus. Crown 8vo, 8s. 6d.

    The Three Sevens. Crown 8vo, 5s. 6d.

    The Millennium; or, the Mystery of God Finished. Crown 8vo, 6s.

A. K. H. B.—From a Quiet Place. A New Volume of Sermons. Crown 8vo, 5s.

ALLEN, Rev. R., M.A.—Abraham: his Life, Times, and Travels, 3800 years ago. With Map. Second Edition. Post 8vo, 6s.

ALLIES, T. W., M.A.—Per Crucem ad Lucem. The Result of a Life. 2 vols. Demy 8vo, 25s.

    A Life's Decision. Crown 8vo, 7s. 6d.

AMOS, Professor Sheldon.—The History and Principles of the Civil Law of Rome. An aid to the Study of Scientific and Comparative Jurisprudence. Demy 8vo. 16s.

ANDERDON, Rev. W. H.—Fasti Apostolici; a Chronology of the Years between the Ascension of our Lord and the Martyrdom of SS. Peter and Paul. Second Edition. Crown 8vo, 2s. 6d.

    Evenings with the Saints. Crown 8vo, 5s.

ARMSTRONG, Richard A., B.A.—Latter-Day Teachers. Six Lectures. Small crown 8vo, 2s. 6d.

AUBERTIN, J. J.—**A Flight to Mexico.** With Seven full-page Illustrations and a Railway Map of Mexico. Crown 8vo, 7s. 6d.

BADGER, George Percy, D.C.L.—**An English-Arabic Lexicon.** In which the equivalent for English Words and Idiomatic Sentences are rendered into literary and colloquial Arabic. Royal 4to, £9 9s.

BAGEHOT, Walter.—**The English Constitution.** Third Edition. Crown 8vo, 7s. 6d.

Lombard Street. A Description of the Money Market. Eighth Edition. Crown 8vo, 7s. 6d.

Some Articles on the Depreciation of Silver, and Topics connected with it. Demy 8vo, 5s.

BAGENAL, Philip H.—**The American-Irish and their Influence on Irish Politics.** Crown 8vo, 5s.

BAGOT, Alan, C.E.—**Accidents in Mines:** their Causes and Prevention. Crown 8vo, 6s.

The Principles of Colliery Ventilation. Second Edition, greatly enlarged. Crown 8vo, 5s.

BAKER, Sir Sherston, Bart.—**The Laws relating to Quarantine.** Crown 8vo, 12s. 6d.

BALDWIN, Capt. J. H.—**The Large and Small Game of Bengal and the North-Western Provinces of India.** With 18 Illustrations. New and Cheaper Edition. Small 4to, 10s. 6d.

BALLIN, Ada S. and F. L.—**A Hebrew Grammar.** With Exercises selected from the Bible. Crown 8vo, 7s. 6d.

BARCLAY, Edgar.—**Mountain Life in Algeria.** With numerous Illustrations by Photogravure. Crown 4to, 16s.

BARLOW, James H.—**The Ultimatum of Pessimism.** An Ethical Study. Demy 8vo, 6s.

BARNES, William.—**Outlines of Redecraft (Logic).** With English Wording. Crown 8vo, 3s.

BAUR, Ferdinand, Dr. Ph.—**A Philological Introduction to Greek and Latin for Students.** Translated and adapted from the German, by C. KEGAN PAUL, M.A., and E. D. STONE, M.A. Third Edition. Crown 8vo, 6s.

BELLARS, Rev. W.—**The Testimony of Conscience to the Truth and Divine Origin of the Christian Revelation.** Burney Prize Essay. Small crown 8vo, 3s. 6d.

BELLINGHAM, Henry, M.P.—**Social Aspects of Catholicism and Protestantism in their Civil Bearing upon Nations.** Translated and adapted from the French of M. le BARON DE HAULLEVILLE. With a preface by His Eminence CARDINAL MANNING. Second and Cheaper Edition. Crown 8vo, 3s. 6d.

BELLINGHAM H. Belsches Graham.—**Ups and Downs of Spanish Travel.** Second Edition. Crown 8vo. 5*s*.

BENN, Alfred W.—**The Greek Philosophers.** 2 vols. Demy 8vo, 28*s*.

BENT, J. Theodore.—**Genoa:** How the Republic Rose and Fell. With 18 Illustrations. Demy 8vo, 18*s*.

BLOOMFIELD, The Lady.—**Reminiscences of Court and Diplomatic Life.** New and Cheaper Edition. With Frontispiece. Crown 8vo, 6*s*.

BLUNT, The Ven. Archdeacon.—**The Divine Patriot, and other Sermons.** Preached in Scarborough and in Cannes. New and Cheaper Edition. Crown 8vo, 4*s*. 6*d*.

BLUNT, Wilfred S.—**The Future of Islam.** Crown 8vo, 6*s*.

BONWICK, J., F.R.G.S.—**Pyramid Facts and Fancies.** Crown 8vo, 5*s*.

BOUVERIE-PUSEY, S. E. B.—**Permanence and Evolution.** An Inquiry into the Supposed Mutability of Animal Types. Crown 8vo, 5*s*.

BOWEN, H. C., M.A.—**Studies in English.** For the use of Modern Schools. Third Edition. Small crown 8vo, 1*s*. 6*d*.

English Grammar for Beginners. Fcap. 8vo, 1*s*.

BRADLEY, F. H.—**The Principles of Logic.** Demy 8vo, 16*s*.

BRIDGETT, Rev. T. E.—**History of the Holy Eucharist in Great Britain.** 2 vols. Demy 8vo, 18*s*.

BRODRICK, the Hon. G. C.—**Political Studies.** Demy 8vo, 14*s*.

BROOKE, Rev. S. A.—**Life and Letters of the Late Rev. F. W. Robertson, M.A.** Edited by.

    I. Uniform with Robertson's Sermons. 2 vols. With Steel Portrait. 7*s*. 6*d*.
    II. Library Edition. With Portrait. 8vo, 12*s*.
    III. A Popular Edition. In 1 vol., 8vo, 6*s*.

The Fight of Faith. Sermons preached on various occasions. Fifth Edition. Crown 8vo, 7*s*. 6*d*.

The Spirit of the Christian Life. New and Cheaper Edition. Crown 8vo, 5*s*.

Theology in the English Poets.—Cowper, Coleridge, Wordsworth, and Burns. Fifth and Cheaper Edition. Post 8vo, 5*s*.

Christ in Modern Life. Sixteenth and Cheaper Edition. Crown 8vo, 5*s*.

Sermons. First Series. Thirteenth and Cheaper Edition. Crown 8vo, 5*s*.

Sermons. Second Series. Sixth and Cheaper Edition. Crown 8vo, 5*s*.

BROWN, Rev. J. Baldwin, B.A.—**The Higher Life.** Its Reality, Experience, and Destiny. Fifth Edition. Crown 8vo, 5s.

Doctrine of Annihilation in the Light of the Gospel of Love. Five Discourses. Fourth Edition. Crown 8vo, 2s. 6d.

The Christian Policy of Life. A Book for Young Men of Business. Third Edition. Crown 8vo, 3s. 6d.

BROWN, S. Borton, B.A.—**The Fire Baptism of all Flesh;** or, the Coming Spiritual Crisis of the Dispensation. Crown 8vo, 6s.

BROWNBILL, John.—**Principles of English Canon Law.** Part I. General Introduction. Crown 8vo, 6s.

BROWNE, W. R.—**The Inspiration of the New Testament.** With a Preface by the Rev. J. P. NORRIS, D.D. Fcap. 8vo, 2s. 6d.

BURTON, Mrs. Richard.—**The Inner Life of Syria, Palestine, and the Holy Land.** Cheaper Edition in one volume. Large post 8vo. 7s. 6d.

BUSBECQ, Ogier Ghiselin de.—**His Life and Letters.** By CHARLES THORNTON FORSTER, M.A., and F. H. BLACKBURNE DANIELL, M.A. 2 vols. With Frontispieces. Demy 8vo, 24s.

CARPENTER, W. B., LL.D., M.D., F.R.S., etc.—**The Principles of Mental Physiology.** With their Applications to the Training and Discipline of the Mind, and the Study of its Morbid Conditions. Illustrated. Sixth Edition. 8vo, 12s.

CERVANTES.—**The Ingenious Knight Don Quixote de la Mancha.** A New Translation from the Originals of 1605 and 1608. By A. J. DUFFIELD. With Notes. 3 vols. Demy 8vo, 42s.

Journey to Parnassus. Spanish Text, with Translation into English Tercets, Preface, and Illustrative Notes, by JAMES Y. GIBSON. Crown 8vo, 12s.

CHEYNE, Rev. T. K.—**The Prophecies of Isaiah.** Translated with Critical Notes and Dissertations. 2 vols. Second Edition. Demy 8vo, 25s.

CLAIRAUT.—**Elements of Geometry.** Translated by Dr. KAINES. With 145 Figures. Crown 8vo, 4s. 6d.

CLAYDEN, P. W.—**England under Lord Beaconsfield.** The Political History of the Last Six Years, from the end of 1873 to the beginning of 1880. Second Edition, with Index and continuation to March, 1880. Demy 8vo, 16s.

Samuel Sharpe. Egyptologist and Translator of the Bible. Crown 8vo, 6s.

CLIFFORD, Samuel.—**What Think Ye of Christ?** Crown 8vo. 6s.

CLODD, Edward, F.R.A.S.—**The Childhood of the World:** a Simple Account of Man in Early Times. Seventh Edition. Crown 8vo, 3s.

A Special Edition for Schools. 1s.

CLOD, Edward, F.R.A.S.—continued.
 The Childhood of Religions. Including a Simple Account of the Birth and Growth of Myths and Legends. Eighth Thousand. Crown 8vo, 5*s.*
  A Special Edition for Schools. 1*s.* 6*d.*
 Jesus of Nazareth. With a brief sketch of Jewish History to the Time of His Birth. Small crown 8vo, 6*s.*

COGHLAN, J. Cole, D.D.—The Modern Pharisee and other Sermons. Edited by the Very Rev. H. H. DICKINSON, D.D., Dean of Chapel Royal, Dublin. New and Cheaper Edition. Crown 8vo, 7*s.* 6*d.*

COLERIDGE, Sara.—Memoir and Letters of Sara Coleridge. Edited by her Daughter. With Index. Cheap Edition. With Portrait. 7*s.* 6*d.*

Collects Exemplified. Being Illustrations from the Old and New Testaments of the Collects for the Sundays after Trinity. By the Author of "A Commentary on the Epistles and Gospels." Edited by the Rev. JOSEPH JACKSON. Crown 8vo, 5*s.*

CONNELL, A. K.—Discontent and Danger in India. Small crown 8vo, 3*s.* 6*d.*
 The Economic Revolution of India. Crown 8vo, 5*s.*

CORY, William.—A Guide to Modern English History. Part I.—MDCCCXV.-MDCCCXXX. Demy 8vo, 9*s.* Part II.—MDCCCXXX.-MDCCCXXXV., 15*s.*

COTTERILL, H. B.—An Introduction to the Study of Poetry. Crown 8vo, 7*s.* 6*d.*

COX, Rev. Sir George W., M.A., Bart.—A History of Greece from the Earliest Period to the end of the Persian War. New Edition. 2 vols. Demy 8vo, 36*s.*
 The Mythology of the Aryan Nations. New Edition. Demy 8vo, 16*s.*
 Tales of Ancient Greece. New Edition. Small crown 8vo, 6*s.*
 A Manual of Mythology in the form of Question and Answer. New Edition. Fcap. 8vo, 3*s.*
 An Introduction to the Science of Comparative Mythology and Folk-Lore. Second Edition. Crown 8vo. 7*s.* 6*d.*

COX, Rev. Sir G. W., M.A., Bart., and JONES, Eustace Hinton.—Popular Romances of the Middle Ages. Second Edition, in 1 vol. Crown 8vo, 6*s.*

COX, Rev. Samuel, D.D.—Salvator Mundi ; or, Is Christ the Saviour of all Men? Eighth Edition. Crown 8vo, 5*s.*
 The Genesis of Evil, and other Sermons, mainly expository. Third Edition. Crown 8vo, 6*s.*

COX, Rev. Samuel, D.D.—continued.
   A Commentary on the Book of Job. With a Translation. Demy 8vo, 15s.
   The Larger Hope. A Sequel to "Salvator Mundi." 16mo, 1s.

CRAVEN, Mrs.—A Year's Meditations. Crown 8vo, 6s.

CRAWFURD, Oswald.—Portugal, Old and New. With Illustrations and Maps. New and Cheaper Edition. Crown 8vo, 6s.

CROZIER, John Beattie, M.B.—The Religion of the Future. Crown 8vo, 6s.

Cyclopædia of Common Things. Edited by the Rev. Sir GEORGE W. Cox, Bart., M.A. With 500 Illustrations. Third Edition. Large post 8vo, 7s. 6d.

DAVIDSON, Rev. Samuel, D.D., LL.D.—Canon of the Bible: Its Formation, History, and Fluctuations. Third and Revised Edition. Small crown 8vo, 5s.
   The Doctrine of Last Things contained in the New Testament compared with the Notions of the Jews and the Statements of Church Creeds. Small crown 8vo, 3s. 6d.

DAVIDSON, Thomas.—The Parthenon Frieze, and other Essays. Crown 8vo, 6s.

DAWSON, Geo., M.A. Prayers, with a Discourse on Prayer. Edited by his Wife. Eighth Edition. Crown 8vo, 6s.
   Sermons on Disputed Points and Special Occasions. Edited by his Wife. Fourth Edition. Crown 8vo, 6s.
   Sermons on Daily Life and Duty. Edited by his Wife. Fourth Edition. Crown 8vo, 6s.
   The Authentic Gospel. A New Volume of Sermons. Edited by GEORGE ST. CLAIR. Third Edition. Crown 8vo, 6s.
   Three Books of God: Nature, History, and Scripture. Sermons edited by GEORGE ST. CLAIR. Crown 8vo, 6s.

DE JONCOURT, Madame Marie.—Wholesome Cookery. Crown 8vo, 3s. 6d.

DE LONG, Lieut. Com. G. W.—The Voyage of the Jeannette. The Ship and Ice Journals of. Edited by his Wife, EMMA DE LONG. With Portraits, Maps, and many Illustrations on wood and stone. 2 vols. Demy 8vo. 36s.

DESPREZ, Phillip S., B.D.—Daniel and John; or, the Apocalypse of the Old and that of the New Testament. Demy 8vo, 12s.

DOWDEN, Edward, LL.D.—Shakspere: a Critical Study of his Mind and Art. Sixth Edition. Post 8vo, 12s.
   Studies in Literature, 1789-1877. Second and Cheaper Edition. Large post 8vo, 6s.

DUFFIELD, A. J.—Don Quixote: his Critics and Commentators. With a brief account of the minor works of MIGUEL DE CERVANTES SAAVEDRA, and a statement of the aim and end of the greatest of them all. A handy book for general readers. Crown 8vo, 3s. 6d.

DU MONCEL, Count.—The Telephone, the Microphone, and the Phonograph. With 74 Illustrations. Second Edition. Small crown 8vo, 5s.

EDGEWORTH, F. Y.—Mathematical Psychics. An Essay on the Application of Mathematics to Social Science. Demy 8vo, 7s. 6d.

Educational Code of the Prussian Nation, in its Present Form. In accordance with the Decisions of the Common Provincial Law, and with those of Recent Legislation. Crown 8vo, 2s. 6d.

Education Library. Edited by PHILIP MAGNUS :—

An Introduction to the History of Educational Theories. By OSCAR BROWNING, M.A. Second Edition. 3s. 6d.

Old Greek Education. By the Rev. Prof. MAHAFFY, M.A. 3s. 6d.

School Management. Including a general view of the work of Education, Organization and Discipline. By JOSEPH LANDON. Second Edition. 6s.

Eighteenth Century Essays. Selected and Edited by AUSTIN DOBSON. With a Miniature Frontispiece by R. Caldecott. Parchment Library Edition, 6s.; vellum, 7s. 6d.

ELSDALE, Henry.—Studies in Tennyson's Idylls. Crown 8vo, 5s.

ELYOT, Sir Thomas.—The Boke named the Gouernour. Edited from the First Edition of 1531 by HENRY HERBERT STEPHEN CROFT, M.A., Barrister-at-Law. With Portraits of Sir Thomas and Lady Elyot, copied by permission of her Majesty from Holbein's Original Drawings at Windsor Castle. 2 vols. Fcap. 4to, 50s.

Enoch the Prophet. The Book of. Archbishop LAURENCE'S Translation, with an Introduction by the Author of "The Evolution of Christianity." Crown 8vo, 5s.

Eranus. A Collection of Exercises in the Alcaic and Sapphic Metres. Edited by F. W. CORNISH, Assistant Master at Eton. Crown 8vo, 2s.

EVANS, Mark.—The Story of Our Father's Love, told to Children. Sixth and Cheaper Edition. With Four Illustrations. Fcap. 8vo, 1s. 6d.

EVANS, Mark—continued.
A Book of Common Prayer and Worship for Household Use, compiled exclusively from the Holy Scriptures. Second Edition. Fcap. 8vo, 1s.

The Gospel of Home Life. Crown 8vo, 4s. 6d.

The King's Story-Book. In Three Parts. Fcap. 8vo, 1s. 6d. each.

⁎⁎ Parts I. and II. with Eight Illustrations and Two Picture Maps, now ready.

"Fan Kwae" at Canton before Treaty Days 1825-1844. By an old Resident. With Frontispiece. Crown 8vo, 5s.

FLECKER, Rev. Eliezer.—Scripture Onomatology. Being Critical Notes on the Septuagint and other versions. Crown 8vo, 3s. 6d.

FLOREDICE, W. H.—A Month among the Mere Irish. Small crown 8vo, 5s.

GARDINER, Samuel R., and J. BASS MULLINGER, M.A.—Introduction to the Study of English History. Large Crown 8vo, 9s.

GARDNER, Dorsey.—Quatre Bras, Ligny, and Waterloo. A Narrative of the Campaign in Belgium, 1815. With Maps and Plans. Demy 8vo, 16s.

Genesis in Advance of Present Science. A Critical Investigation of Chapters I.-IX. By a Septuagenarian Beneficed Presbyter. Demy 8vo. 10s. 6d.

GENNA, E.—Irresponsible Philanthropists. Being some Chapters on the Employment of Gentlewomen. Small crown 8vo, 2s. 6d.

GEORGE, Henry.—Progress and Poverty : An Inquiry into the Causes of Industrial Depressions, and of Increase of Want with Increase of Wealth. The Remedy. Second Edition. Post 8vo, 7s. 6d. Also a Cheap Edition. Limp cloth, 1s. 6d. Paper covers, 1s.

GIBSON, James Y.—Journey to Parnassus. Composed by MIGUEL DE CERVANTES SAAVEDRA. Spanish Text, with Translation into English Tercets, Preface, and Illustrative Notes, by. Crown 8vo, 12s.

Glossary of Terms and Phrases. Edited by the Rev. H. PERCY SMITH and others. Medium 8vo, 12s.

GLOVER, F., M.A.—Exempla Latina. A First Construing Book, with Short Notes, Lexicon, and an Introduction to the Analysis of Sentences. Fcap. 8vo, 2s.

GOLDSMID, Sir Francis Henry, Bart., Q.C., M.P.—Memoir of. With Portrait. Second Edition, Revised. Crown 8vo, 6s.

GOODENOUGH, *Commodore J. G.*—Memoir of, with Extracts from his Letters and Journals. Edited by his Widow. With Steel Engraved Portrait. Square 8vo, 5s.

⁎ Also a Library Edition with Maps, Woodcuts, and Steel Engraved Portrait. Square post 8vo, 14s.

GOSSE, *Edmund W.*—Studies in the Literature of Northern Europe. With a Frontispiece designed and etched by Alma Tadema. New and Cheaper Edition. Large crown 8vo, 6s.

Seventeenth Century Studies. A Contribution to the History of English Poetry. Demy 8vo, 10s. 6d.

GOULD, *Rev. S. Baring, M.A.*—Germany, Present and Past. New and Cheaper Edition. Large crown 8vo, 7s. 6d.

GOWAN, *Major Walter E.*—A. Ivanoff's Russian Grammar. (16th Edition.) Translated, enlarged, and arranged for use of Students of the Russian Language. Demy 8vo, 6s.

GOWER, *Lord Ronald.* My Reminiscences. Second Edition. 2 vols. With Frontispieces. Demy 8vo, 30s.

GRAHAM, *William, M.A.*—The Creed of Science, Religious, Moral, and Social. Demy 8vo, 6s.

GRIFFITH, *Thomas, A.M.*—The Gospel of the Divine Life: a Study of the Fourth Evangelist. Demy 8vo, 14s.

GRIMLEY, *Rev. H. N., M.A.*—Tremadoc Sermons, chiefly on the Spiritual Body, the Unseen World, and the Divine Humanity. Third Edition. Crown 8vo, 6s.

HAECKEL, *Prof. Ernst.*—The History of Creation. Translation revised by Professor E. RAY LANKESTER, M.A., F.R.S. With Coloured Plates and Genealogical Trees of the various groups of both Plants and Animals. 2 vols. Third Edition. Post 8vo, 32s.

The History of the Evolution of Man. With numerous Illustrations. 2 vols. Post 8vo, 32s.

A Visit to Ceylon. Post 8vo, 7s. 6d.

Freedom in Science and Teaching. With a Prefatory Note by T. H. HUXLEY, F.R.S. Crown 8vo, 5s.

HALF-CROWN SERIES:—

A Lost Love. By ANNA C. OGLE [Ashford Owen].

Sister Dora: a Biography. By MARGARET LONSDALE.

True Words for Brave Men: a Book for Soldiers and Sailors. By the late CHARLES KINGSLEY.

An Inland Voyage. By R. L. STEVENSON.

Travels with a Donkey. By R. L. STEVENSON.

HALF-CROWN SERIES—*continued.*

Notes of Travel : being Extracts from the Journals of Count VON MOLTKE.

English Sonnets. Collected and Arranged by J. DENNIS.

London Lyrics. By F. LOCKER.

Home Songs for Quiet Hours. By the Rev. Canon R. H. BAYNES.

HAWEIS, Rev. H. R., M.A.—**Current Coin.** Materialism—The Devil—Crime—Drunkenness—Pauperism—Emotion—Recreation—The Sabbath. Fifth and Cheaper Edition. Crown 8vo, 5s.

Arrows in the Air. Fifth and Cheaper Edition. Crown 8vo, 5s.

Speech in Season. Fifth and Cheaper Edition. Crown 8vo, 5s.

Thoughts for the Times. Thirteenth and Cheaper Edition. Crown 8vo, 5s.

Unsectarian Family Prayers. New and Cheaper Edition. Fcap. 8vo, 1s. 6d.

HAWKINS, Edwards Comerford.—**Spirit and Form.** Sermons preached in the Parish Church of Leatherhead. Crown 8vo, 6s.

HAWTHORNE, Nathaniel.—**Works.** Complete in Twelve Volumes. Large post 8vo, 7s. 6d. each volume.

- VOL. I. TWICE-TOLD TALES.
- II. MOSSES FROM AN OLD MANSE.
- III. THE HOUSE OF THE SEVEN GABLES, AND THE SNOW IMAGE.
- IV. THE WONDERBOOK, TANGLEWOOD TALES, AND GRANDFATHER'S CHAIR.
- V. THE SCARLET LETTER, AND THE BLITHEDALE ROMANCE.
- VI. THE MARBLE FAUN. [Transformation.]
- VII.
- VIII. } OUR OLD HOME, AND ENGLISH NOTE-BOOKS.
- IX. AMERICAN NOTE-BOOKS.
- X. FRENCH AND ITALIAN NOTE-BOOKS.
- XI. SEPTIMIUS FELTON, THE DOLLIVER ROMANCE, FANSHAWE, AND, IN AN APPENDIX, THE ANCESTRAL FOOTSTEP.
- XII. TALES AND ESSAYS, AND OTHER PAPERS, WITH A BIOGRAPHICAL SKETCH OF HAWTHORNE.

HAYES, A. H., Junr.—**New Colorado, and the Santa Fé Trail.** With Map and 60 Illustrations. Crown 8vo, 9s.

HENNESSY, Sir John Pope.—**Ralegh in Ireland.** With his Letters on Irish Affairs and some Contemporary Documents. Large crown 8vo, printed on hand-made paper, parchment, 10s. 6d.

HENRY, Philip.—**Diaries and Letters of.** Edited by MATTHEW HENRY LEE, M.A. Large crown 8vo, 7s. 6d.

HIDE, Albert.—**The Age to Come.** Small crown 8vo, 2s. 6d.

HIME, Major H. W. L., R.A.—**Wagnerism : A Protest.** Crown 8vo, 2*s.* 6*d.*

HINTON, J.—**Life and Letters.** Edited by ELLICE HOPKINS, with an Introduction by Sir W. W. GULL, Bart., and Portrait engraved on Steel by C. H. Jeens. Fourth Edition. Crown 8vo, 8*s.* 6*d.*

The Mystery of Pain. New Edition. Fcap. 8vo, 1*s.*

HOLTHAM, E. G.—**Eight Years in Japan, 1873-1881.** Work, Travel, and Recreation. With three maps. Large crown 8vo, 9*s.*

HOOPER, Mary.—**Little Dinners : How to Serve them with Elegance and Economy.** Seventeenth Edition. Crown 8vo, 2*s.* 6*d.*

Cookery for Invalids, Persons of Delicate Digestion, and Children. Third Edition. Crown 8vo, 2*s.* 6*d.*

Every-Day Meals. Being Economical and Wholesome Recipes for Breakfast, Luncheon, and Supper. Fifth Edition. Crown 8vo, 2*s.* 6*d.*

HOPKINS, Ellice.—**Life and Letters of James Hinton,** with an Introduction by Sir W. W. GULL, Bart., and Portrait engraved on Steel by C. H. Jeens. Fourth Edition. Crown 8vo, 8*s.* 6*d.*

Work amongst Working Men. Fourth edition. Crown 8vo, 3*s.* 6*d.*

HOSPITALIER, E.—**The Modern Applications of Electricity.** Translated and Enlarged by JULIUS MAIER, Ph.D. 2 vols. With numerous Illustrations. Demy 8vo, 12*s.* 6*d.* each volume.

VOL. I.—Electric Generators, Electric Light.
VOL. II.—Telephone : Various Applications : Electrical Transmission of Energy.

Household Readings on Prophecy. By a Layman. Small crown 8vo, 3*s.* 6*d.*

HUGHES, Henry.—**The Redemption of the World.** Crown 8vo, 3*s.* 6*d.*

HUNTINGFORD, Rev. E., D.C.L.—**The Apocalypse.** With a Commentary and Introductory Essay. Demy 8vo, 9*s.*

HUTTON, Arthur, M.A.—**The Anglican Ministry : Its Nature and Value** in relation to the Catholic Priesthood. With a Preface by His Eminence CARDINAL NEWMAN. Demy 8vo, 14*s.*

HUTTON, Rev. C. F.—**Unconscious Testimony ;** or, the Silent Witness of the Hebrew to the Truth of the Historical Scriptures. Crown 8vo, 2*s.* 6*d.*

IM THURN, Everard F.—**Among the Indians of British Guiana.** Being Sketches, chiefly anthropologic, from the Interior of British Guiana. With numerous Illustrations. Demy 8vo.

JENKINS, E., and RAYMOND, J.—The Architect's Legal Handbook. Third Edition, Revised. Crown 8vo, 6s.

JENKINS, Rev. R. C., M.A.—The Privilege of Peter, and the Claims of the Roman Church confronted with the Scriptures, the Councils, and the Testimony of the Popes themselves. Fcap. 8vo, 3s. 6d.

JERVIS, Rev. W. Henley.—The Gallican Church and the Revolution. A Sequel to the History of the Church of France, from the Concordat of Bologna to the Revolution. Demy 8vo, 18s.

JOEL, L.—A Consul's Manual and Shipowner's and Shipmaster's Practical Guide in their Transactions Abroad. With Definitions of Nautical, Mercantile, and Legal Terms; a Glossary of Mercantile Terms in English, French, German, Italian, and Spanish; Tables of the Money, Weights, and Measures of the Principal Commercial Nations and their Equivalents in British Standards; and Forms of Consular and Notarial Acts. Demy 8vo, 12s.

JOHNSTONE, C. F., M.A.—Historical Abstracts: being Outlines of the History of some of the less known States of Europe. Crown 8vo, 7s. 6d.

JOLLY, William, F.R.S.E., etc.—The Life of John Duncan, Scotch Weaver and Botanist. With Sketches of his Friends and. Notices of his Times. Second Edition. Large crown 8vo, with etched portrait, 9s.

JONES, C. A.—The Foreign Freaks of Five Friends. With 30 Illustrations. Crown 8vo, 6s.

JOYCE, P. W., LL.D., etc.—Old Celtic Romances. Translated from the Gaelic. Crown 8vo, 7s. 6d.

JOYNES, J. L.—The Adventures of a Tourist in Ireland. Second edition. Small crown 8vo, 2s. 6d.

KAUFMANN, Rev. M., B.A.—Socialism: its Nature, its Dangers, and its Remedies considered. Crown 8vo, 7s. 6d.

Utopias; or, Schemes of Social Improvement, from Sir Thomas More to Karl Marx. Crown 8vo, 5s.

KAY, Joseph.—Free Trade in Land. Edited by his Widow. With Preface by the Right Hon. JOHN BRIGHT, M.P. Sixth Edition. Crown 8vo, 5s.

KEMPIS, Thomas à.—Of the Imitation of Christ. Parchment Library Edition, 6s.; or vellum, 7s. 6d. The Red Line Edition, fcap. 8vo, red edges, 2s. 6d. The Cabinet Edition, small 8vo, cloth limp, 1s.; cloth boards, red edges, 1s. 6d. The Miniature Edition, red edges, 32mo, 1s.

⁎⁎⁎ All the above Editions may be had in various extra bindings.

KENT, C.—Corona Catholica ad Petri successoris Pedes Oblata: De Summi Pontificis Leonis XIII. Assumptione Epigramma. In Quinquaginta Linguis. Fcap. 4to, 15s.

KETTLEWELL, Rev. S.—Thomas à Kempis and the Brothers of Common Life. 2 vols. With Frontispieces. Demy 8vo, 30s.

KIDD, Joseph, M.D.—The Laws of Therapeutics; or, the Science and Art of Medicine. Second Edition. Crown 8vo, 6s.

KINGSFORD, Anna, M.D.—The Perfect Way in Diet. A Treatise advocating a Return to the Natural and Ancient Food of our Race. Small crown 8vo, 2s.

KINGSLEY, Charles, M.A.—Letters and Memories of his Life. Edited by his Wife. With two Steel Engraved Portraits, and Vignettes on Wood. Thirteenth Cabinet Edition. 2 vols. Crown 8vo, 12s.

** Also a New and Condensed Edition, in one volume. With Portrait. Crown 8vo, 6s.

All Saints' Day, and other Sermons. Also a new and condensed Edition in one volume, with Portrait. Crown 8vo, 6s. Edited by the Rev. W. HARRISON. Third Edition. Crown 8vo, 7s. 6d.

True Words for Brave Men. A Book for Soldiers' and Sailors' Libraries. Tenth Edition. Crown 8vo, 2s. 6d.

KNOX, Alexander A.—The New Playground; or, Wanderings in Algeria. New and cheaper edition. Large crown 8vo, 6s.

LANDON Joseph.—School Management; Including a General View of the Work of Education, Organization, and Discipline. Second Edition. Crown 8vo, 6s.

LAURIE, S. S.—The Training of Teachers, and other Educational Papers. Crown 8vo, 7s. 6d.

LEE, Rev. F. G., D.C.L.—The Other World; or, Glimpses of the Supernatural. 2 vols. A New Edition. Crown 8vo, 15s.

Letters from a Young Emigrant in Manitoba. Second Edition. Small crown 8vo, 3s. 6d.

LEWIS, Edward Dillon.—A Draft Code of Criminal Law and Procedure. Demy 8vo, 21s.

LILLIE, Arthur, M.R.A.S.—The Popular Life of Buddha. Containing an Answer to the Hibbert Lectures of 1881. With Illustrations. Crown 8vo, 6s.

LINDSAY, W. Lauder, M.D.—Mind in the Lower Animals in Health and Disease. 2 vols. Demy 8vo, 32s.

Vol. I.—Mind in Health. Vol. II.—Mind in Disease.

LLOYD, Walter.—The Hope of the World: An Essay on Universal Redemption. Crown 8vo, 5s.

LONSDALE, Margaret.—Sister Dora: a Biography. With Portrait. Twenty-fifth Edition. Crown 8vo, 2s. 6d.

LOWDER, Charles.—A Biography. By the Author of " St. Teresa." New and Cheaper Edition. Crown 8vo. With Portrait. 3s. 6d.

LYTTON, Edward Bulwer, Lord.—Life, Letters and Literary Remains. By his Son, The EARL OF LYTTON. With Portraits, Illustrations and Facsimiles. Demy 8vo.
[Vols. I. and II. just ready.

MACHIAVELLI, Niccolò.—Discourses on the First Decade of Titus Livius. Translated from the Italian by NINIAN HILL THOMSON, M.A. Large crown 8vo, 12*s.*

The Prince. Translated from the Italian by N. H. T. Small crown 8vo, printed on hand-made paper, bevelled boards, 6*s.*

MACKENZIE, Alexander.—How India is Governed. Being an Account of England's Work in India. Small crown 8vo, 2*s.*

MACNAUGHT, Rev. John.—Cœna Domini : An Essay on the Lord's Supper, its Primitive Institution, Apostolic Uses, and Subsequent History. Demy 8vo, 14*s.*

MACWALTER, Rev. G. S.—Life of Antonis Rosmini Serbati (Founder of the Institute of Charity). 2 vols. Demy 8vo.
[Vol. I. now ready, price 12*s.*

MAGNUS, Mrs.—About the Jews since Bible Times. From the Babylonian Exile till the English Exodus. Small crown 8vo, 6*s.*

MAIR, R. S., M.D., F.R.C.S.E.—The Medical Guide for Anglo-Indians. Being a Compendium of Advice to Europeans in India, relating to the Preservation and Regulation of Health. With a Supplement on the Management of Children in India. Second Edition. Crown 8vo, limp cloth, 3*s.* 6*d.*

MALDEN, Henry Elliot.—Vienna, 1683. The History and Consequences of the Defeat of the Turks before Vienna, September 12th, 1683, by John Sobieski, King of Poland, and Charles Leopold, Duke of Lorraine. Crown 8vo, 4*s.* 6*d.*

Many Voices. A volume of Extracts from the Religious Writers of Christendom from the First to the Sixteenth Century. With Biographical Sketches. Crown 8vo, cloth extra, red edges, 6*s.*

MARKHAM, Capt. Albert Hastings, R.N.—The Great Frozen Sea : A Personal Narrative of the Voyage of the *Alert* during the Arctic Expedition of 1875-6. With 6 Full-page Illustrations, 2 Maps, and 27 Woodcuts. Sixth and Cheaper Edition. Crown 8vo, 6*s.*

A Polar Reconnaissance : being the Voyage of the *Isbjörn* to Novaya Zemlya in 1879. With 10 Illustrations. Demy 8vo, 16*s.*

Marriage and Maternity ; or, Scripture Wives and Mothers. Small crown 8vo, 4*s.* 6*d.*

MARTINEAU, Gertrude.—Outline Lessons on Morals. Small crown 8vo, 3*s.* 6*d.*

MAUDSLEY, H., M.D.—Body and Will. Being an Essay concerning Will, in its Metaphysical, Physiological, and Pathological Aspects. 8vo, 12*s.*

McGRATH, Terence.—Pictures from Ireland. New and Cheaper Edition. Crown 8vo, 2s.

MEREDITH, M.A.—Theotokos, the Example for Woman. Dedicated, by permission, to Lady Agnes Wood. Revised by the Venerable Archdeacon DENISON. 32mo, limp cloth, 1s. 6d.

MILLER, Edward.—The History and Doctrines of Irvingism; or, the so-called Catholic and Apostolic Church. 2 vols. Large post 8vo, 25s.

The Church in Relation to the State. Large crown 8vo, 7s. 6d.

MINCHIN, J. G.—Bulgaria since the War : Notes of a Tour in the Autumn of 1879. Small crown 8vo, 3s. 6d.

MITFORD, Bertram.—Through the Zulu Country. Its Battlefields and its People. With five Illustrations. Demy 8vo, 14s.

MIVART, St. George.—Nature and Thought: An Introduction to a Natural Philosophy. Demy 8vo, 10s. 6d.

MOCKLER, E.—A Grammar of the Baloochee Language, as it is spoken in Makran (Ancient Gedrosia), in the Persia-Arabic and Roman characters. Fcap. 8vo, 5s.

MOLESWORTH, Rev. W. Nassau, M.A.—History of the Church of England from 1660. Large crown 8vo, 7s. 6d.

MORELL, J. R.—Euclid Simplified in Method and Language. Being a Manual of Geometry. Compiled from the most important French Works, approved by the University of Paris and the Minister of Public Instruction. Fcap. 8vo, 2s. 6d.

MORSE, E. S., Ph.D.—First Book of Zoology. With numerous Illustrations. New and Cheaper Edition. Crown 8vo, 2s. 6d.

MURPHY, John Nicholas.—The Chair of Peter; or, the Papacy considered in its Institution, Development, and Organization, and in the Benefits which for over Eighteen Centuries it has conferred on Mankind. Demy 8vo, 18s.

NELSON, J. H., M.A.—A Prospectus of the Scientific Study of the Hindû Law. Demy 8vo, 9s.

NEWMAN, J. H., D.D.—Characteristics from the Writings of. Being Selections from his various Works. Arranged with the Author's personal Approval. Sixth Edition. With Portrait. Crown 8vo, 6s.

** A Portrait of Cardinal Newman, mounted for framing, can be had, 2s. 6d.

NEWMAN, Francis William.—Essays on Diet. Small crown 8vo, cloth limp, 2s.

New Werther. By LOKI. Small crown 8vo, 2s. 6d.

NICHOLSON, Edward Byron.—The Gospel according to the Hebrews. Its Fragments Translated and Annotated with a Critical Analysis of the External and Internal Evidence relating to it. Demy 8vo, 9s. 6d.

A New Commentary on the Gospel according to Matthew. Demy 8vo, 12s.

NICOLS, Arthur, F.G.S., F.R.G.S.—Chapters from the Physical History of the Earth: an Introduction to Geology and Palæontology. With numerous Illustrations. Crown 8vo, 5s.

NOPS, Marianne.—Class Lessons on Euclid. Part I. containing the First two Books of the Elements. Crown 8vo, 2s. 6d.

Notes on St. Paul's Epistle to the Galatians. For Readers of the Authorized Version or the Original Greek. Demy 8vo, 2s. 6d.

Nuces: EXERCISES ON THE SYNTAX OF THE PUBLIC SCHOOL LATIN PRIMER. New Edition in Three Parts. Crown 8vo, each 1s.
⁎ The Three Parts can also be had bound together, 3s.

OATES, Frank, F.R.G.S.—Matabele Land and the Victoria Falls. A Naturalist's Wanderings in the Interior of South Africa. Edited by C. G. OATES, B.A. With numerous Illustrations and 4 Maps. Demy 8vo, 21s.

OGLE, W., M.D., F.R.C.P.—Aristotle on the Parts of Animals. Translated, with Introduction and Notes. Royal 8vo, 12s. 6d.

Oken Lorenz, Life of. By ALEXANDER ECKER. With Explanatory Notes, Selections from Oken's Correspondence, and Portrait of the Professor. From the German by ALFRED TULK. Crown 8vo, 6s.

O'MEARA, Kathleen.—Frederic Ozanam, Professor of the Sorbonne: His Life and Work. Second Edition. Crown 8vo, 7s. 6d.

Henri Perreyve and his Counsels to the Sick. Small crown 8vo, 5s.

OSBORNE, Rev. W. A.—The Revised Version of the New Testament. A Critical Commentary, with Notes upon the Text. Crown 8vo, 5s.

OTTLEY, H. Bickersteth.—The Great Dilemma. Christ His Own Witness or His Own Accuser. Six Lectures. Second Edition. Crown 8vo, 3s. 6d.

Our Public Schools—Eton, Harrow, Winchester, Rugby, Westminster, Marlborough, The Charterhouse. Crown 8vo, 6s.

OWEN, F. M.—John Keats: a Study. Crown 8vo, 6s.

OWEN, Rev. Robert, B.D.—Sanctorale Catholicum; or, Book of Saints. With Notes, Critical, Exegetical, and Historical. Demy 8vo, 18s.

OXENHAM, Rev. F. Nutcombe.—What is the Truth as to Everlasting Punishment. Part II. Being an Historical Inquiry into the Witness and Weight of certain Anti-Origenist Councils. Crown 8vo, 2s. 6d.

OXONIENSES.—Romanism, Protestantism, Anglicanism. Being a Layman's View of some questions of the Day. Together with Remarks on Dr. Littledale's "Plain Reasons against joining the Church of Rome." Crown 8vo, 3s. 6d.

PALMER, the late William.—Notes of a Visit to Russia in 1840-1841. Selected and arranged by JOHN H. CARDINAL NEWMAN, with portrait. Crown 8vo, 8s. 6d.

Parchment Library. Choicely Printed on hand-made paper, limp parchment antique, 6s. ; vellum, 7s. 6d. each volume.

English Lyrics.

The Sonnets of John Milton. Edited by MARK PATTISON. With Portrait after Vertue.

Poems by Alfred Tennyson. 2 vols. With minature frontispieces by W. B. Richmond.

French Lyrics. Selected and Annotated by GEORGE SAINTSBURY. With a minature frontispiece designed and etched by H. G. Glindoni.

The Fables of Mr. John Gay. With Memoir by AUSTIN DOBSON, and an etched portrait from an unfinished Oil Sketch by Sir Godfrey Kneller.

Select Letters of Percy Bysshe Shelley. Edited, with an Introduction, by RICHARD GARNETT.

The Christian Year. Thoughts in Verse for the Sundays and Holy Days throughout the Year. With Miniature Portrait of the Rev. J. Keble, after a Drawing by G. Richmond, R.A.

Shakspere's Works. Complete in Twelve Volumes.

Eighteenth Century Essays. Selected and Edited by AUSTIN DOBSON. With a Miniature Frontispiece by R. Caldecott.

Q. Horati Flacci Opera. Edited by F. A. CORNISH, Assistant Master at Eton. With a Frontispiece after a design by L. Alma Tadema, etched by Leopold Lowenstam.

Edgar Allan Poe's Poems. With an Essay on his Poetry by ANDREW LANG, and a Frontispiece by Linley Sambourne.

Shakspere's Sonnets. Edited by EDWARD DOWDEN. With a Frontispiece etched by Leopold Lowenstam, after the Death Mask.

English Odes. Selected by EDMUND W. GOSSE. With Frontispiece on India paper by Hamo Thornycroft, A.R.A.

Of the Imitation of Christ. By THOMAS À KEMPIS. A revised Translation. With Frontispiece on India paper, from a Design by W. B. Richmond.

Parchment Library—*continued*.
    Tennyson's The Princess: a Medley. With a Miniature Frontispiece by H. M. Paget, and a Tailpiece in Outline by Gordon Browne.
    Poems: Selected from PERCY BYSSHE SHELLEY. Dedicated to Lady Shelley. With a Preface by RICHARD GARNETT and a Miniature Frontispiece.
    Tennyson's "In Memoriam." With a Miniature Portrait in *eau-forte* by Le Rat, after a Photograph by the late Mrs. Cameron.

PARSLOE, Joseph.—Our Railways. Sketches, Historical and Descriptive. With Practical Information as to Fares and Rates, etc., and a Chapter on Railway Reform. Crown 8vo, 6s.

PAUL, C. Kegan.—Biographical Sketches. Printed on hand-made paper, bound in buckram. Second Edition. Crown 8vo, 7s. 6d.

PAUL, Alexander.—Short Parliaments. A History of the National Demand for frequent General Elections. Small crown 8vo, 3s. 6d.

PEARSON, Rev. S.—Week-day Living. A Book for Young Men and Women. Second Edition. Crown 8vo, 5s.

PENRICE, Maj. J., B.A.—A Dictionary and Glossary of the Ko-ran. With Copious Grammatical References and Explanations of the Text. 4to, 21s.

PESCHEL, Dr. Oscar.—The Races of Man and their Geographical Distribution. Large crown 8vo, 9s.

PETERS, F. H.—The Nicomachean Ethics of Aristotle. Translated by. Crown 8vo, 6s.

PHIPSON, E.—The Animal Lore of Shakspeare's Time. Including Quadrupeds, Birds, Reptiles, Fish and Insects. Large post 8vo, 9s.

PIDGEON, D.—An Engineer's Holiday; or, Notes of a Round Trip from Long. 0° to 0°. New and Cheaper Edition. Large crown 8vo, 7s. 6d.

PRICE, Prof. Bonamy.—Currency and Banking. Crown 8vo, 6s.
    Chapters on Practical Political Economy. Being the Substance of Lectures delivered before the University of Oxford. New and Cheaper Edition. Large post 8vo, 5s.

Pulpit Commentary, The. (Old Testament Series.) Edited by the Rev. J. S. EXELL and the Rev. Canon H. D. M. SPENCE.
    Genesis. By the Rev. T. WHITELAW, M.A.; with Homilies by the Very Rev. J. F. MONTGOMERY, D.D., Rev. Prof. R. A. REDFORD, M.A., LL.B., Rev. F. HASTINGS, Rev. W. ROBERTS, M.A. An Introduction to the Study of the Old Testament by the Venerable Archdeacon FARRAR, D.D., F.R.S.; and Introductions to the Pentateuch by the Right Rev. H. COTTERILL, D.D., and Rev. T. WHITELAW, M.A. Seventh Edition. 1 vol., 15s.

Pulpit Commentary, The—*continued.*

Exodus. By the Rev. Canon RAWLINSON. With Homilies by Rev. J. ORR, Rev. D. YOUNG, Rev. C. A. GOODHART, Rev. J. URQUHART, and the Rev. H. T. ROBJOHNS. Third Edition. 2 vols., 18s.

Leviticus. By the Rev. Prebendary MEYRICK, M.A. With Introductions by the Rev. R. COLLINS, Rev. Professor A. CAVE, and Homilies by Rev. Prof. REDFORD, LL.B., Rev. J. A. MACDONALD, Rev. W. CLARKSON, Rev. S. R. ALDRIDGE, LL.B., and Rev. MCCHEYNE EDGAR. Fourth Edition. 15s.

Numbers. By the Rev. R. WINTERBOTHAM, LL.B.; with Homilies by the Rev. Professor W. BINNIE, D.D., Rev. E. S. PROUT, M.A., Rev. D. YOUNG, Rev. J. WAITE, and an Introduction by the Rev. THOMAS WHITELAW, M.A. Fourth Edition. 15s.

Deuteronomy. By the Rev. W. L. ALEXANDER, D.D. With Homilies by Rev. C. CLEMANCE, D.D., Rev. J. ORR, B.D., Rev. R. M. EDGAR, M.A., Rev. D. DAVIES, M.A. Third edition. 15s.

Joshua. By Rev. J. J. LIAS, M.A.; with Homilies by Rev. S. R. ALDRIDGE, LL.B., Rev. R. GLOVER, REV. E. DE PRESSENSÉ, D.D., Rev. J. WAITE, B.A., Rev. F. W. ADENEY, M.A.; and an Introduction by the Rev. A. PLUMMER, M.A. Fifth Edition. 12s. 6d.

Judges and Ruth. By the Bishop of Bath and Wells, and Rev. J. MORRISON, D.D.; with Homilies by Rev. A. F. MUIR, M.A., Rev. W. F. ADENEY, M.A., Rev. W. M. STATHAM, and Rev. Professor J. THOMSON, M.A. Fourth Edition. 10s. 6d.

1 Samuel. By the Very Rev. R. P. SMITH, D.D.; with Homilies by Rev. DONALD FRASER, D.D., Rev. Prof. CHAPMAN, and Rev. B. DALE. Sixth Edition. 15s.

1 Kings. By the Rev. JOSEPH HAMMOND, LL.D. With Homilies by the Rev. E. DE PRESSENSÉ, D.D., Rev. J. WAITE, B.A., Rev. A. ROWLAND, LL.B., Rev. J. A. MACDONALD, and Rev. J. URQUHART. Fourth Edition. 15s.

Ezra, Nehemiah, and Esther. By Rev. Canon G. RAWLINSON, M.A.; with Homilies by Rev. Prof. J. R. THOMSON, M.A., Rev. Prof. R. A. REDFORD, LL.B., M.A., Rev. W. S. LEWIS, M.A., Rev. J. A. MACDONALD, Rev. A. MACKENNAL, B.A., Rev. W. CLARKSON, B.A., Rev. F. HASTINGS, Rev. W. DINWIDDIE, LL.B., Rev. Prof. ROWLANDS, B.A., Rev. G. WOOD, B.A., Rev. Prof. P. C. BARKER, LL.B., M.A., and the Rev. J. S. EXELL. Sixth Edition. 1 vol., 12s. 6d.

Jeremiah. By the Rev. J. K. CHEYNE, M.A.; with Homilies by the Rev. W. F. ADENEY, M.A., Rev. A. F. MUIR, M.A., Rev. S. CONWAY, B.A., Rev. J. WAITE, B.A., and Rev. D. YOUNG, B.A. Vol. I., 15s.

Pulpit Commentary, The. (New Testament Series.)
St. Mark. By Very Rev. E. BICKERSTETH, D.D., Dean of Lichfield; with Homilies by Rev. Prof. THOMSON, M.A., Rev. Prof. GIVEN, M.A., Rev. Prof. JOHNSON, M.A., Rev. A. ROWLAND, B.A., LL.B., Rev. A. MUIR, and Rev. R. GREEN. 2 vols. Third Edition. 21s.

PUSEY, Dr.—Sermons for the Church's Seasons from Advent to Trinity. Selected from the Published Sermons of the late EDWARD BOUVERIE PUSEY, D.D. Crown 8vo, 5s.

QUILTER, Harry.—"The Academy," 1872–1882.

RADCLIFFE, Frank R. Y.—The New Politicus. Small crown 8vo, 2s. 6d.

Realities of the Future Life. Small crown 8vo, 1s. 6d.

RENDELL, J. M.—Concise Handbook of the Island of Madeira. With Plan of Funchal and Map of the Island. Fcap. 8vo, 1s. 6d.

REYNOLDS, Rev. J. W.—The Supernatural in Nature. A Verification by Free Use of Science. Third Edition, Revised and Enlarged. Demy 8vo, 14s.

The Mystery of Miracles. Third and Enlarged Edition. Crown 8vo, 6s.

RIBOT, Prof. Th.—Heredity: A Psychological Study on its Phenomena, its Laws, its Causes, and its Consequences. Large crown 8vo, 9s.

ROBERTSON, The late Rev. F. W., M.A.—Life and Letters of. Edited by the Rev. STOPFORD BROOKE, M.A.
 I. Two vols., uniform with the Sermons. With Steel Portrait. Crown 8vo, 7s. 6d.
 II. Library Edition, in Demy 8vo, with Portrait. 12s.
 III. A Popular Edition, in 1 vol. Crown 8vo, 6s.

Sermons. Four Series. Small crown 8vo, 3s. 6d. each.

The Human Race, and other Sermons. Preached at Cheltenham, Oxford, and Brighton. New and Cheaper Edition. Crown 8vo, 3s. 6d.

Notes on Genesis. New and Cheaper Edition. Crown 8vo, 3s. 6d.

Expository Lectures on St. Paul's Epistles to the Corinthians. A New Edition. Small crown 8vo, 5s.

Lectures and Addresses, with other Literary Remains. A New Edition. Crown 8vo, 5s.

An Analysis of Mr. Tennyson's "In Memoriam." (Dedicated by Permission to the Poet-Laureate.) Fcap. 8vo, 2s.

The Education of the Human Race. Translated from the German of GOTTHOLD EPHRAIM LESSING. Fcap. 8vo, 2s. 6d.

The above Works can also be had, bound in half morocco.

⁎⁎* A Portrait of the late Rev. F. W. Robertson, mounted for framing, can be had, 2s. 6d.

Rosmini Serbati (Life of). By G. STUART MACWALTER. 2 vols. 8vo. [Vol. I. now ready, 12s.

Rosmini's Origin of Ideas. Translated from the Fifth Italian Edition of the Nuovo Saggio *Sull' origine delle idee*. 3 vols. Demy 8vo, cloth. [Vols. I. and II. now ready, 16s. each.

Rosmini's Philosophical System. Translated, with a Sketch of the Author's Life, Bibliography, Introduction, and Notes by THOMAS DAVIDSON. Demy 8vo, 16s.

RULE, Martin, M.A.—The Life and Times of St. Anselm, Archbishop of Canterbury and Primate of the Britains. 2 vols. Demy 8vo, 21s.

SALVATOR, Archduke Ludwig.—Levkosia, the Capital of Cyprus. Crown 4to, 10s. 6d.

SAMUEL, Sydney M.—Jewish Life in the East. Small crown 8vo, 3s. 6d.

SAYCE, Rev. Archibald Henry.—Introduction to the Science of Language. 2 vols. Second Edition. Large post 8vo, 25s.

Scientific Layman. The New Truth and the Old Faith: are they Incompatible? Demy 8vo, 10s. 6d.

SCOONES, W. Baptiste.—Four Centuries of English Letters: A Selection of 350 Letters by 150 Writers, from the Period of the Paston Letters to the Present Time. Third Edition. Large crown 8vo, 6s.

SHILLITO, Rev. Joseph.—Womanhood: its Duties, Temptations, and Privileges. A Book for Young Women. Third Edition. Crown 8vo, 3s. 6d.

SHIPLEY, Rev. Orby, M.A.—Principles of the Faith in Relation to Sin. Topics for Thought in Times of Retreat. Eleven Addresses delivered during a Retreat of Three Days to Persons living in the World. Demy 8vo, 12s.

Sister Augustine, Superior of the Sisters of Charity at the St. Johannis Hospital at Bonn. Authorised Translation by HANS THARAU, from the German "Memorials of AMALIE VON LASAULX." Cheap Edition. Large crown 8vo, 4s. 6d.

SMITH, Edward, M.D., LL.B., F.R.S.—Tubercular Consumption in its Early and Remediable Stages. Second Edition. Crown 8vo, 6s.

SPEDDING, James.—Reviews and Discussions, Literary, Political, and Historical not relating to Bacon. Demy 8vo, 12s. 6d.

Evenings with a Reviewer; or, Bacon and Macaulay. With a Prefatory Notice by G. S. VENABLES, Q.C. 2 vols. Demy 8vo, 18s.

STAPFER, Paul.—Shakspeare and Classical Antiquity: Greek and Latin Antiquity as presented in Shakspeare's Plays. Translated by EMILY J. CAREY. Large post 8vo, 12s.

STEVENSON, Rev. W. F.—Hymns for the Church and Home. Selected and Edited by the Rev. W. FLEMING STEVENSON. The Hymn Book consists of Three Parts:—I. For Public Worship.—II. For Family and Private Worship.—III. For Children.

*** Published in various forms and prices, the latter ranging from 8d. to 6s.
Lists and full particulars will be furnished on application to the Publishers.

STEVENSON, Robert Louis.—Travels with a Donkey in the Cevennes. With Frontispiece by Walter Crane. Small crown 8vo, 2s. 6d.

An Inland Voyage. With Frontispiece by Walter Crane. Small Crown 8vo, 2s. 6d.

Virginibus Puerisque, and other Papers. Crown 8vo, 6s.

Stray Papers on Education, and Scenes from School Life. By B. H. Small crown 8vo, 3s. 6d.

STRECKER-WISLICENUS.—Organic Chemistry. Translated and Edited, with Extensive Additions, by W. R. HODGKINSON, Ph.D., and A. J. GREENAWAY, F.I.C. Demy 8vo, 21s.

SULLY, James, M.A.—Pessimism: a History and a Criticism. Second Edition. Demy 8vo, 14s.

SWEDENBORG, Eman.—De Cultu et Amore Dei ubi Agitur de Telluris ortu, Paradiso et Vivario, tum de Primogeniti Seu Adami Nativitate Infantia, et Amore. Crown 8vo, 5s.

SYME, David.—Representative Government in England. Its Faults and Failures. Second Edition. Large crown 8vo, 6s.

TAYLOR, Rev. Isaac.—The Alphabet. An Account of the Origin and Development of Letters. With numerous Tables and Facsimiles. 2 vols. Demy 8vo, 36s.

Thirty Thousand Thoughts. Edited by the Rev. CANON SPENCE, Rev. J. S. EXELL, Rev. CHARLES NEIL, and Rev. JACOB STEPHENSON. 6 vols. Super royal 8vo.
[Vol. I. now ready, 16s.

THOM, J. Hamilton.—Laws of Life after the Mind of Christ. Second Edition. Crown 8vo, 7s. 6d.

THOMSON, J. Turnbull.—Social Problems; or, An Inquiry into the Laws of Influence. With Diagrams. Demy 8vo, 10s. 6d.

TIDMAN, Paul F.—Gold and Silver Money. Part I.—A Plain Statement. Part II.—Objections Answered. Third Edition. Crown 8vo, 1s.

TIPPLE, Rev. S. A.—Sunday Mornings at Norwood. Prayers and Sermons. Crown 8vo, 6s.

TODHUNTER, Dr. J.—A Study of Shelley. Crown 8vo, 7s.

TREMENHEERE, Hugh Seymour, C.B.—A Manual of the Principles of Government, as set forth by the Authorities of Ancient and Modern Times. New and Enlarged Edition. Crown 8vo, 5s.

TUKE, Daniel Hack, M.D., F.R.C.P.—Chapters in the History of the Insane in the British Isles. With 4 Illustrations. Large crown 8vo, 12s.

TWINING, Louisa.—Workhouse Visiting and Management during Twenty-Five Years. Small crown 8vo, 3s. 6d.

TYLER, J.—The Mystery of Being: or, What Do We Know? Small crown 8vo, 3s. 6d.

UPTON, Major R. D.—Gleanings from the Desert of Arabia. Large post 8vo, 10s. 6d.

VACUUS, Viator.—Flying South. Recollections of France and its Littoral. Small crown 8vo, 3s. 6d.

VAUGHAN, H. Halford.—New Readings and Renderings of Shakespeare's Tragedies. 2 vols. Demy 8vo, 25s.

VILLARI, Professor.—Niccolò Machiavelli and his Times. Translated by Linda Villari. 4 vols. Large post 8vo, 48s.

VILLIERS, The Right Hon. C. P.—Free Trade Speeches of. With Political Memoir. Edited by a Member of the Cobden Club. 2 vols. With Portrait. Demy 8vo, 25s.

VOGT, Lieut.-Col. Hermann.—The Egyptian War of 1882. A translation. With Map and Plans. Large crown 8vo, 6s.

VOLCKXSOM, E. W. V.—Catechism of Elementary Modern Chemistry. Small crown 8vo, 3s.

VYNER, Lady Mary.—Every Day a Portion. Adapted from the Bible and the Prayer Book, for the Private Devotion of those living in Widowhood. Collected and Edited by Lady Mary Vyner. Square crown 8vo, 5s.

WALDSTEIN, Charles, Ph.D.—The Balance of Emotion and Intellect; an Introductory Essay to the Study of Philosophy. Crown 8vo, 6s.

WALLER, Rev. C. B.—The Apocalypse, reviewed under the Light of the Doctrine of the Unfolding Ages, and the Restitution of All Things. Demy 8vo, 12s.

WALPOLE, Chas. George.—History of Ireland from the Earliest Times to the Union with Great Britain. With 5 Maps and Appendices. Crown 8vo, 10s. 6d.

WALSHE, Walter Hayle, M.D.—Dramatic Singing Physiologically Estimated. Crown 8vo, 3s. 6d.

WEDMORE, Frederick.—The Masters of Genre Painting. With Sixteen Illustrations. Crown 8vo, 7s. 6d.

WHEWELL, William, D.D.—His Life and Selections from his Correspondence. By Mrs. STAIR DOUGLAS. With a Portrait from a Painting by Samuel Laurence. Demy 8vo, 21s.

WHITNEY, Prof. William Dwight.—Essentials of English Grammar, for the Use of Schools. Crown 8vo, 3s. 6d.

WILLIAMS, Rowland, D.D.—Psalms, Litanies, Counsels, and Collects for Devout Persons. Edited by his Widow. New and Popular Edition. Crown 8vo, 3s. 6d.

Stray Thoughts Collected from the Writings of the late Rowland Williams, D.D. Edited by his Widow. Crown 8vo, 3s. 6d.

WILLIS, R., M.A.—William Harvey. A History of the Discovery of the Circulation of the Blood: with a Portrait of Harvey after Faithorne. Demy 8vo, 14s.

WILSON, Sir Erasmus.—Egypt of the Past. With Chromo-lithograph and numerous Illustrations in the text. Second Edition, Revised. Crown 8vo, 12s.

The Recent Archaic Discovery of Egyptian Mummies at Thebes. A Lecture. Crown 8vo, 1s. 6d.

WILSON, Lieut.-Col. C. T.—The Duke of Berwick, Marshall of France, 1702-1734. Demy 8vo, 15s.

WOLTMANN, Dr. Alfred, and WOERMANN, Dr. Karl.—History of Painting. Edited by SIDNEY COLVIN. Vol. I. Painting in Antiquity and the Middle Ages. With numerous Illustrations. Medium 8vo, 28s.; bevelled boards, gilt leaves, 30s.

Word was Made Flesh. Short Family Readings on the Epistles for each Sunday of the Christian Year. Demy 8vo, 10s. 6d.

WREN, Sir Christopher.—His Family and His Times. With Original Letters, and a Discourse on Architecture hitherto unpublished. By LUCY PHILLIMORE. With Portrait. Demy 8vo, 14s.

YOUMANS, Eliza A.—First Book of Botany. Designed to Cultivate the Observing Powers of Children. With 300 Engravings. New and Cheaper Edition. Crown 8vo, 2s. 6d.

YOUMANS, Edward L., M.D.—A Class Book of Chemistry, on the Basis of the New System. With 200 Illustrations. Crown 8vo, 5s.

the world drowned the still small voice of reason and conscience in its appeals to men's better judgment and feelings.

But in order to be fair and just we must remember that Socrates and men of his stamp touch their contemporaries in a very tender part. Socrates admits that his mode of addressing his contemporaries was unpleasant to them, but then he alleges that it was a sort of medicine which was good for them. This they did not perceive; its present flavour and quality were disagreeable, and roused a feeling of hostility, and there did not exist at Athens, and there has not existed elsewhere amongst the common people generally, an openness of mind, a calmness of temper, and a judicial faculty which would enable them to weigh and measure the statements put before them. There has been no disposition to do this. "Am I become your enemy because I tell you the truth?" asks St Paul, but this in the main is what people did, and do think, whenever that which the speaker calls truth happens to conflict with what the hearer has been accustomed to consider the truth. If we would do justice to the Athenians we must take account of this general infirmity of mankind, and then we shall have to ask ourselves also whether the Athenians were more or less tenacious and intemperate in their opposition and resistance to new teachers than their neighbours. There was, then, this antagonism between Socrates and a large part of the Athenians, mixed up also, as it may be assumed, with some political feeling, of which there was not a little in Athens. Socrates, be it remembered, was one of that party who thought that the functions of government belonged legitimately to those who knew best how to exercise them for the good of the governed. *NB* The legitimate king or governor was not the man who held the sceptre, nor the man elected by some vulgar persons, nor he who had got the post by lot, nor he who had thrust himself in by force or fraud; but he alone who knew how to govern well ; just as the pilot governed on shipboard, and the surgeon in a sick man's house, and the trainer in the palæstra, simply because their greater knowledge was an admitted fact. It was absurd, Socrates contended, to choose political officers by lot, when no one would trust himself on shipboard under care of a pilot picked up by chance. Under these circumstances, a time came when his opponents determined to bring him before the tribunal, and the mode of doing it was this : Athens at that time was governed by ten Archons. One of these was called the King Archon, and his functions were almost all connected with religion. He was, as his title shows, the representative of the old kings in their capacity of high priest, and had to offer up sacrifices and prayer ;

XXXII. **General Physiology of Muscles and Nerves.** By Prof. J. Rosenthal. Third Edition. With Illustrations. Crown 8vo, 5s.

XXXIII. **Sight:** an Exposition of the Principles of Monocular and Binocular Vision. By Joseph le Conte, LL.D. Second Edition. With 132 Illustrations. Crown 8vo, 5s.

XXXIV. **Illusions:** a Psychological Study. By James Sully. Second Edition. Crown 8vo, 5s.

XXXV. **Volcanoes: what they are and what they teach.** By Professor J. W. Judd, F.R.S. With 92 Illustrations on Wood. Second Edition. Crown 8vo, 5s.

XXXVI. **Suicide:** an Essay in Comparative Moral Statistics. By Prof. E. Morselli. Second Edition. With Diagrams. Crown 8vo, 5s.

XXXVII. **The Brain and its Functions.** By J. Luys. With Illustrations. Second Edition. Crown 8vo, 5s.

XXXVIII. **Myth and Science:** an Essay. By Tito Vignoli. Crown 8vo, 5s.

XXXIX. **The Sun.** By Professor Young. With Illustrations. Second Edition. Crown 8vo, 5s.

XL. **Ants, Bees, and Wasps:** a Record of Observations on the Habits of the Social Hymenoptera. By Sir John Lubbock, Bart., M.P. With 5 Chromo-lithographic Illustrations. Sixth Edition. Crown 8vo, 5s.

XLI. **Animal Intelligence.** By G. J. Romanes, LL.D., F.R.S. Third Edition. Crown 8vo, 5s.

XLII. **The Concepts and Theories of Modern Physics.** By J. B. Stallo. Second Edition. Crown 8vo, 5s.

XLIII. **Diseases of the Memory;** An Essay in the Positive Psychology. By Prof. Th. Ribot. Second Edition. Crown 8vo, 5s.

XLIV. **Man before Metals.** By N. Joly, with 148 Illustrations. Third Edition. Crown 8vo, 5s.

XLV. **The Science of Politics.** By Prof. Sheldon Amos. Second Edition. Crown 8vo, 5s.

XLVI. **Elementary Meteorology.** By Robert H. Scott. Second Edition. With Numerous Illustrations. Crown 8vo, 5s.

XLVII. **The Organs of Speech and their Application in the Formation of Articulate Sounds.** By George Hermann Von Meyer. With 47 Woodcuts. Crown 8vo, 5s.

XLVIII. **Fallacies.** A View of Logic from the Practical Side. By Alfred Sidgwick.

MILITARY WORKS.

BARRINGTON, Capt. J. T.—**England on the Defensive**; or, the Problem of Invasion Critically Examined. Large crown 8vo, with Map, 7s. 6d.

BRACKENBURY, Col. C. B., R.A., C.B.—**Military Handbooks for Regimental Officers.**

    I. **Military Sketching and Reconnaissance.** By Col. F. J. Hutchison, and Major H. G. MacGregor. Fourth Edition. With 15 Plates. Small 8vo, 6s.

    II. **The Elements of Modern Tactics Practically applied to English Formations.** By Lieut.-Col. Wilkinson Shaw. Fourth Edition. With 25 Plates and Maps. Small crown 8vo, 9s.

    III. **Field Artillery.** Its Equipment, Organization and Tactics. By Major Sisson C. Pratt, R.A. With 12 Plates. Second Edition. Small crown 8vo, 6s.

    IV. **The Elements of Military Administration.** First Part : Permanent System of Administration. By Major J. W. Buxton. Small crown 8vo. 7s. 6d.

    V. **Military Law:** Its Procedure and Practice. By Major Sisson C. Pratt, R.A. Small crown 8vo.

BROOKE, Major, C. K.—**A System of Field Training.** Small crown 8vo, cloth limp, 2s.

CLERY, C., Lieut.-Col.—**Minor Tactics.** With 26 Maps and Plans. Sixth and Cheaper Edition, Revised. Crown 8vo, 9s.

COLVILE, Lieut.-Col. C. F.—**Military Tribunals.** Sewed, 2s. 6d.

HARRISON, Lieut.-Col. R.—**The Officer's Memorandum Book for Peace and War.** Third Edition. Oblong 32mo, roan, with pencil, 3s. 6d.

Notes on Cavalry Tactics, Organisation, etc. By a Cavalry Officer. With Diagrams. Demy 8vo, 12s.

PARR, Capt. H. Hallam, C.M.G.—**The Dress, Horses, and Equipment of Infantry and Staff Officers.** Crown 8vo, 1s.

SCHAW, Col. H.—**The Defence and Attack of Positions and Localities.** Second Edition, Revised and Corrected. Crown 8vo, 3s. 6d.

SHADWELL, Maj.-Gen., C.B.—**Mountain Warfare.** Illustrated by the Campaign of 1799 in Switzerland. Being a Translation of the Swiss Narrative compiled from the Works of the Archduke Charles, Jomini, and others. Also of Notes by General H. Dufour on the Campaign of the Valtelline in 1635. With Appendix, Maps, and Introductory Remarks. Demy 8vo, 16s.

they are jealous of all of us. I suppose we must be brave and not mind them.

Soc. Their laughter, friend Euthyphro, is not a matter of much consequence. For a man may be thought wise; but the Athenians, I suspect, do not care much about this, until he begins to make other men wise; and then, for some reason or other—perhaps, as you say, from jealousy—they are angry.

Euth. I have no desire to try conclusions with them about this.

Soc. I dare say you don't make yourself common, and are not apt to impart your wisdom. But I have a benevolent habit of pouring out myself to everybody, and would even pay for a listener, and I am afraid the Athenians know this; and therefore, as I was saying, if the Athenians would only laugh at me as you say they laugh at you, the time might pass gaily enough in the court; but perhaps they may be in earnest, and then what the end may be you soothsayers only can predict.

Euth. I dare say the affair will end in nothing, Socrates, and that you will win your cause; and I think I shall win mine.

Soc. By the powers, Euthyphro! how little does the common herd know of the nature of right and truth!

Euth. And how little do they know, Socrates, of the opinions of the gods about piety and impiety.

Soc. Good Heavens, Euthyphro! have you any precise knowledge of piety and impiety, and of divine things in general?

Euth. The best of Euthyphro, and that which distinguishes him, Socrates, from other men, is his exact knowledge of all these matters.

Soc. Rare friend! I think I cannot do better than be your disciple before the trial with Melêtus comes on. Then I shall challenge him, and say that I have always had a great interest in all religious questions, and now, as he charges me with rash imaginations and innovations in religion, I have become your disciple. I suppose that people think me wrong because I cannot believe all the current stories about the gods. But as you are so well informed about them and approve them, I cannot do better than assent to your superior wisdom. What else can I do, confessing as I must that I know nothing of them? I wish you would tell me whether you really believe that they are true.

Euth. Yes, Socrates; and things more wonderful still of which the world is in ignorance.

Soc. And do you really believe that the gods fought with one another, and had dire quarrels, battles, and the like, as the poets say, and as you may find represented in the works of great artists? The temples are full of them; and notably the robe of Athene, which is carried up to the Acropolis at the great Panathenæa, is embroidered with them. Are all these tales of the gods true, Euthyphro?

Euth. Yes, Socrates.

The conversation is carried on much further, until Euthyphro says at last:—

I really do not know, Socrates, how to say what I mean, for somehow or other our arguments, on whatever ground we rest them, seem to turn round and walk away.

Euthyphro was one of those superficial and self-satisfied people who are as numerous in the world now as they were then. Socrates flatters his vanity in order that he may convince him of his ignorance; but he does not succeed, and the conversation ends as it began, leaving Euthyphro with the same good opinion

EDMONDS, E. W.—Hesperas. Rhythm and Rhyme. Crown 8vo, 4*s.*

ELDRYTH, Maud.—Margaret, and other Poems. Small crown 8vo, 3*s.* 6*d.*

ELLIOTT, Ebenezer, The Corn Law Rhymer.—Poems. Edited by his son, the Rev. EDWIN ELLIOTT, of St. John's, Antigua. 2 vols. Crown 8vo, 18*s.*

English Odes. Selected, with a Critical Introduction by EDMUND W. GOSSE, and a miniature frontispiece by Hamo Thornycroft, A.R.A. Elzevir 8vo, limp parchment antique, 6*s.*; vellum, 7*s.* 6*d.*

EVANS, Anne.—Poems and Music. With Memorial Preface by ANN THACKERAY RITCHIE. Large crown 8vo, 7*s.*

GOSSE, Edmund W.—New Poems. Crown 8vo, 7*s.* 6*d.*

GRAHAM, William. Two Fancies and other Poems. Crown 8vo, 5*s.*

GRINDROD, Charles. Plays from English History. Crown 8vo, 7*s.* 6*d.*

GURNEY, Rev. Alfred.—The Vision of the Eucharist, and other Poems. Crown 8vo, 5*s.*

HELLON, H. G.—Daphnis: a Pastoral Poem. Small crown 8vo, 3*s.* 6*d.*

Herman Waldgrave: a Life's Drama. By the Author of "Ginevra," etc. Crown 8vo, 6*s.*

HICKEY, E. H.—A Sculptor, and other Poems. Small crown 8vo, 5*s.*

Horati Opera. Edited by F. A. CORNISH, Assistant Master at Eton. With a Frontispiece after a design by L. Alma Tadema, etched by Leopold Lowenstam. Parchment Library Edition, 6*s.*; vellum, 7*s.* 6*d.*

INGHAM, Sarson, C. J.—Cædmon's Vision, and other Poems. Small crown 8vo, 5*s.*

JENKINS, Rev. Canon.—Alfonso Petrucci, Cardinal and Conspirator: an Historical Tragedy in Five Acts. Small crown 8vo, 3*s.* 6*d.*

KING, Edward.—Echoes from the Orient. With Miscellaneous Poems. Small crown 8vo, 3*s.* 6*d.*

KING, Mrs. Hamilton.—The Disciples. Fifth Edition, with Portrait and Notes. Crown 8vo, 5*s.*

    A Book of Dreams. Crown 8vo, 5*s.*

LANG, A.—XXXII Ballades in Blue China. Elzevir 8vo, parchment, 5*s.*

LAWSON, Right Hon. Mr. Justice.—Hymni Usitati Latine Redditi : with other Verses. Small 8vo, parchment, 5s.

LEIGH, Arran and Isla.—Bellerophon. Small crown 8vo, 5s.

LEIGHTON, Robert.—Records, and other Poems. With Portrait. Small crown 8vo, 7s. 6d.

Lessings Nathan the Wise. Translated by EUSTACE K. CORBETT. Crown 8vo, 6s.

Living English Poets MDCCCLXXXII. With Frontispiece by Walter Crane. Second Edition. Large crown 8vo. Printed on hand-made paper. Parchment, 12s., vellum, 15s.

LOCKER, F.—London Lyrics. A New and Cheaper Edition. Small crown 8vo, 2s. 6d.

Love in Idleness. A Volume of Poems. With an etching by W. B. Scott. Small crown 8vo, 5s.

Love Sonnets of Proteus. With Frontispiece by the Author. Elzevir 8vo, 5s.

LOWNDES, Henry.—Poems and Translations. Crown 8vo, 6s.

LUMSDEN, Lieut.-Col. H. W.—Beowulf : an Old English Poem. Translated into Modern Rhymes. Second Edition. Small crown 8vo, 5s.

Lyre and Star. Poems by the Author of "Ginevra," etc. Crown 8vo, 5s.

MACLEAN, Charles Donald.—Latin and Greek Verse Translations. Small crown 8vo, 2s.

MAGNUSSON, Eirikr, M.A., and PALMER, E. H., M.A.—Johan Ludvig Runeberg's Lyrical Songs, Idylls, and Epigrams. Fcap. 8vo, 5s.

M.D.C.—Chronicles of Christopher Columbus. A Poem in Twelve Cantos. Crown 8vo, 7s. 6d.

MEREDITH, Owen, The Earl of Lytton.—Lucile. New Edition. With 32 Illustrations. 16mo, 3s. 6d. Cloth extra, gilt edges, 4s. 6d.

MIDDLETON, The Lady.—Ballads. Square 16mo, 3s. 6d.

MORICE, Rev. F. D., M.A.—The Olympian and Pythian Odes of Pindar. A New Translation in English Verse. Crown 8vo, 7s. 6d.

MORRIS, Lewis.—Poetical Works of. New and Cheaper Editions, with Portrait. Complete in 3 vols., 5s. each.
    Vol. I. contains "Songs of Two Worlds." Vol. II. contains "The Epic of Hades." Vol. III. contains "Gwen" and "The Ode of Life."

MORRIS, Lewis—continued.

The Epic of Hades. With 16 Autotype Illustrations, after the Drawings of the late George R. Chapman. 4to, cloth extra, gilt leaves, 25*s.*

The Epic of Hades. Presentation Edition. 4to, cloth extra, gilt leaves, 10*s.* 6*d.*

Ode of Life, The. Fourth Edition. Crown 8vo, 5*s.*

Songs Unsung. Fcap. 8vo.

MORSHEAD, E. D. A.—The House of Atreus. Being the Agamemnon, Libation-Bearers, and Furies of Æschylus. Translated into English Verse. Crown 8vo, 7*s.*

The Suppliant Maidens of Æschylus. Crown 8vo, 3*s.* 6*d.*

NADEN, Constance W.—Songs and Sonnets of Spring Time. Small crown 8vo, 5*s.*

NEWELL, E. J.—The Sorrows of Simona and Lyrical Verses. Small crown 8vo, 3*s.* 6*d.*

NOAKE, Major R. Compton.—The Bivouac; or, Martial Lyrist. With an Appendix: Advice to the Soldier. Fcap. 8vo, 5*s.* 6*d.*

NOEL, The Hon. Roden.—A Little Child's Monument. Second Edition. Small crown 8vo, 3*s.* 6*d.*

NORRIS, Rev. Alfred.—The Inner and Outer Life. Poems. Fcap. 8vo, 6*s.*

O'HAGAN, John.—The Song of Roland. Translated into English Verse. New and Cheaper Edition. Crown 8vo, 5*s.*

PFEIFFER, Emily.—Glan Alarch: His Silence and Song: a Poem. Second Edition. Crown 8vo, 6*s.*

Gerard's Monument, and other Poems. Second Edition. Crown 8vo, 6*s.*

Quarterman's Grace, and other Poems. Crown 8vo, 5*s.*

Poems. Second Edition. Crown 8vo, 6*s.*

Sonnets and Songs. New Edition. 16mo, handsomely printed and bound in cloth, gilt edges, 4*s.*

Under the Aspens; Lyrical and Dramatic. With Portrait. Crown 8vo, 6*s.*

PIKE, Warburton.—The Inferno of Dante Allighieri. Demy 8vo, 5*s.*

POE, Edgar Allan.—Poems. With an Essay on his Poetry by ANDREW LANG, and a Frontispiece by Linley Sambourne. Parchment Library Edition, 6*s.*; vellum, 7*s.* 6*d.*

Rare Poems of the 16th and 17th Centuries. Edited W. J. LINTON. Crown 8vo, 5s.

RHOADES, James.—**The Georgics of Virgil.** Translated into English Verse. Small crown 8vo, 5s.

ROBINSON, A. Mary F.—**A Handful of Honeysuckle.** Fcap. 8vo, 3s. 6d.

The Crowned Hippolytus. Translated from Euripides. With New Poems. Small crown 8vo, 5s.

SAUNDERS, John.—**Love's Martyrdom.** A Play and Poem. Small crown 8vo, 5s.

Schiller's Mary Stuart. German Text, with English Translation on opposite page by LEEDHAM WHITE. Crown 8vo, 6s.

SCOTT, George F. E.—**Theodora and other Poems.** Small 8vo, 3s. 6d.

SELKIRK, J. B.—**Poems.** Crown 8vo, 7s. 6d.

Shakspere's Sonnets. Edited by EDWARD DOWDEN. With a Frontispiece etched by Leopold Lowenstam, after the Death Mask. Parchment Library Edition, 6s.; vellum, 7s. 6d.

Shakspere's Works. Complete in 12 Volumes. Parchment Library Edition, 6s. each; vellum, 7s. 6d. each.

SHAW, W. F., M.A.—**Juvenal, Persius, Martial, and Catullus.** An Experiment in Translation. Crown 8vo, 5s.

SHELLEY, Percy Bysshe.—**Poems Selected from.** Dedicated to Lady Shelley. With Preface by RICHARD GARNETT. Parchment Library Edition, 6s.; vellum, 7s. 6d.

Six Ballads about King Arthur. Crown 8vo, extra, gilt edges, 3s. 6d.

SLADEN, Douglas B.—**Frithjof and Ingebjorg, and other Poems.** Small crown 8vo, 5s.

TAYLOR, Sir H.—**Works.** Complete in Five Volumes. Crown 8vo, 30s.

Philip Van Artevelde. Fcap. 8vo, 3s. 6d.

The Virgin Widow, etc. Fcap. 8vo, 3s. 6d.

The Statesman. Fcap. 8vo, 3s. 6d.

TENNYSON, Alfred.—Works Complete :—

The Imperial Library Edition. Complete in 7 vols. Demy 8vo, 10s. 6d. each; in Roxburgh binding, 12s. 6d. each.

Author's Edition. In 7 vols. Post 8vo, gilt 43s. 6d.; or half-morocco, Roxburgh style, 54s.

Cabinet Edition. 13 vols. Each with Frontispiece. Fcap. 8vo, 2s. 6d. each.

Cabinet Edition. 13 vols. Complete in handsome Ornamental Case. 35s.

TENNYSON, Alfred—continued.

The Royal Edition. In 1 vol. With 26 Illustrations and Portrait. Extra, bevelled boards, gilt leaves, 21*s.*

The Guinea Edition. Complete in 13 vols. neatly bound and enclosed in box, 21*s.* ; French morocco or parchment, 31*s.* 6*d.*

Shilling Edition. In 13 vols. pocket size, 1*s.* each, sewed.

The Crown Edition. Complete in 1 vol. strongly bound, 6*s.* ; extra gilt leaves, 7*s.* 6*d.* ; Roxburgh, half-morocco, 8*s.* 6*d.*

⁎⁎ Can also be had in a variety of other bindings.

In Memoriam. With a Miniature Portrait in *eau-forte* by Le Rat, after a Photograph by the late Mrs. Cameron. Parchment Library Edition, 6*s.* ; vellum, 7*s.* 6*d.*

The Princess. A Medley. With a Miniature Frontispiece by H. M. Paget, and a Tailpiece in Outline by Gordon Browne. Parchment Library Edition, 6*s.* ; vellum, 7*s.* 6*d.*

Original Editions :—

Poems. Small 8vo, 6*s.*

Maud, and other Poems. Small 8vo, 3*s.* 6*d.*

The Princess. Small 8vo, 3*s.* 6*d.*

Idylls of the King. Small 8vo, 5*s.*

Idylls of the King. Complete. Small 8vo, 6*s.*

The Holy Grail, and other Poems. Small 8vo, 4*s.* 6*d.*

Gareth and Lynette. Small 8vo, 3*s.*

Enoch Arden, etc. Small 8vo, 3*s.* 6*d.*

In Memoriam. Small 8vo, 4*s.*

Harold : a Drama. New Edition. Crown 8vo, 6*s.*

Queen Mary : a Drama. New Edition. Crown 8vo, 6*s.*

The Lover's Tale. Fcap. 8vo, 3*s.* 6*d.*

Ballads, and other Poems. Small 8vo, 5*s.*

Selections from the above Works. Super royal 16mo, 3*s.* 6*d.* ; gilt extra, 4*s.*

Songs from the above Works. 16mo, 2*s.* 6*d.*

Tennyson for the Young and for Recitation. Specially arranged. Fcap. 8vo, 1*s.* 6*d.*

The Tennyson Birthday Book. Edited by EMILY SHAKESPEAR. 32mo, limp, 2*s.* ; extra, 3*s.*

⁎⁎ A superior Edition, printed in red and black, on antique paper, specially prepared. Small crown 8vo, extra, gilt leaves, 5*s.* ; and in various calf and morocco bindings.

THORNTON, L. M.—The Son of Shelomith. Small crown 8vo, 3s. 6d.

TODHUNTER, Dr. J.—Laurella, and other Poems. Crown 8vo, 6s. 6d.

 Forest Songs. Small crown 8vo, 3s. 6d.

 The True Tragedy of Rienzi : a Drama. 3s. 6d.

 Alcestis : a Dramatic Poem. Extra fcap. 8vo, 5s.

 A Study of Shelley. Crown 8vo, 7s.

 Translations from Dante, Petrarch, Michael Angelo, and Vittoria Colonna. Fcap. 8vo, 7s. 6d.

TURNER, Rev. C. Tennyson.—Sonnets, Lyrics, and Translations. Crown 8vo, 4s. 6d.

 Collected Sonnets, Old and New. With Prefatory Poem by ALFRED TENNYSON; also some Marginal Notes by S. T. COLERIDGE, and a Critical Essay by JAMES SPEDDING. Fcap. 8vo, 7s. 6d.

WALTERS, Sophia Lydia.—A Dreamer's Sketch Book. With 21 Illustrations by Percival Skelton, R. P. Leitch, W. H. J. Boot, and T. R. Pritchett. Engraved by J. D. Cooper. Fcap. 4to, 12s. 6d.

WEBSTER, Augusta.—In a Day : a Drama. Small crown 8vo, 2s. 6d.

Wet Days. By a Farmer. Small crown 8vo, 6s.

WILKINS, William.—Songs of Study. Crown 8vo, 6s.

WILLIAMS, J.—A Story of Three Years, and other Poems. Small crown 8vo, 3s. 6d.

YOUNGS, Ella Sharpe.—Paphus, and other Poems. Small crown 8vo, 3s. 6d.

WORKS OF FICTION IN ONE VOLUME.

BANKS, Mrs. G. L.—God's Providence House. New Edition. Crown 8vo, 3s. 6d.

HARDY, Thomas.—A Pair of Blue Eyes. Author of "Far from the Madding Crowd." New Edition. Crown 8vo, 6s.

 The Return of the Native. New Edition. With Frontispiece. Crown 8vo, 6s.

INGELOW, Jean.—Off the Skelligs : a Novel. With Frontispiece. Second Edition. Crown 8vo, 6s.

MACDONALD, G.—Castle Warlock. A Novel. New and Cheaper Edition. Crown 8vo, 6s.

MACDONALD, G.—continued.

 Malcolm. With Portrait of the Author engraved on Steel. Sixth Edition. Crown 8vo, 6s.

 The Marquis of Lossie. Fourth Edition. With Frontispiece. Crown 8vo, 6s.

 St. George and St. Michael. Third Edition. With Frontispiece. Crown 8vo, 6s.

PALGRAVE, W. Gifford.—Hermann Agha: an Eastern Narrative. Third Edition. Crown 8vo, 6s.

SHAW, Flora L.—Castle Blair; a Story of Youthful Lives. New and Cheaper Edition. Crown 8vo, 3s. 6d.

STRETTON, Hesba.—Through a Needle's Eye: a Story. New and Cheaper Edition, with Frontispiece. Crown 8vo, 6s.

TAYLOR, Col. Meadows, C.S.I., M.R.I.A.—Seeta: a Novel. New and Cheaper Edition. With Frontispiece. Crown 8vo, 6s.

 Tippoo Sultaun: a Tale of the Mysore War. New Edition, with Frontispiece. Crown 8vo, 6s.

 Ralph Darnell. New and Cheaper Edition. With Frontispiece. Crown 8vo, 6s.

 A Noble Queen. New and Cheaper Edition. With Frontispiece. Crown 8vo, 6s.

 The Confessions of a Thug. Crown 8vo, 6s.

 Tara: a Mahratta Tale. Crown 8vo, 6s.

Within Sound of the Sea. New and Cheaper Edition, with Frontispiece. Crown 8vo, 6s.

BOOKS FOR THE YOUNG.

Brave Men's Footsteps. A Book of Example and Anecdote for Young People. By the Editor of "Men who have Risen." With 4 Illustrations by C. Doyle. Eighth Edition. Crown 8vo, 3s. 6d.

COXHEAD, Ethel.—Birds and Babies. Imp. 16mo. With 33 Illustrations. Cloth gilt, 2s. 6d.

DAVIES, G. Christopher.—Rambles and Adventures of our School Field Club. With 4 Illustrations. New and Cheaper Edition. Crown 8vo, 3s. 6d.

EDMONDS, Herbert.—Well Spent Lives: a Series of Modern Biographies. New and Cheaper Edition. Crown 8vo, 3s. 6d.

EVANS, Mark.—**The Story of our Father's Love,** told to Children. Fourth and Cheaper Edition of Theology for Children. With 4 Illustrations. Fcap. 8vo, 1s. 6d.

JOHNSON, Virginia W.—**The Catskill Fairies.** Illustrated by Alfred Fredericks. 5s.

MAC KENNA, S. J.—**Plucky Fellows.** A Book for Boys. With 6 Illustrations. Fifth Edition. Crown 8vo, 3s. 6d.

REANEY, Mrs. G. S.—**Waking and Working;** or, From Girlhood to Womanhood. New and Cheaper Edition. With a Frontispiece. Crown 8vo, 3s. 6d.

Blessing and Blessed: a Sketch of Girl Life. New and Cheaper Edition. Crown 8vo, 3s. 6d.

Rose Gurney's Discovery. A Book for Girls. Dedicated to their Mothers. Crown 8vo, 3s. 6d.

English Girls: Their Place and Power. With Preface by the Rev. R. W. Dale. Fourth Edition. Fcap. 8vo, 2s. 6d.

Just Anyone, and other Stories. Three Illustrations. Royal 16mo, 1s. 6d.

Sunbeam Willie, and other Stories. Three Illustrations. Royal 16mo, 1s. 6d.

Sunshine Jenny, and other Stories. Three Illustrations. Royal 16mo, 1s. 6d.

STOCKTON, Frank R.—**A Jolly Fellowship.** With 20 Illustrations. Crown 8vo, 5s.

STORR, Francis, and TURNER, Hawes.—**Canterbury Chimes;** or, Chaucer Tales retold to Children. With 6 Illustrations from the Ellesmere MS. Second Edition. Fcap. 8vo, 3s. 6d.

STRETTON, Hesba.—**David Lloyd's Last Will.** With 4 Illustrations. New Edition. Royal 16mo, 2s. 6d.

Tales from Ariosto Re-told for Children. By a Lady. With 3 Illustrations. Crown 8vo, 4s. 6d.

WHITAKER, Florence.—**Christy's Inheritance.** A London Story. Illustrated. Royal 16mo, 1s. 6d.

www.ingramcontent.com/pod-product-compliance
Lightning Source LLC
Chambersburg PA
CBHW031402160426
43196CB00007B/861